SAP R/3 for Everyone

Praise for *SAP R/3 for Everyone*

"T... ...d con-
sist... ...for
beg... ...

...*America*

"S... ...he mys-
ter... ...read
this...

...*Specialist*

"T... ...provide
a w... ...nation.
Th... ...nderful
boo...

...*Manager*

"S... ...epts and
tas... ...more
spe...

...*Learning*

SAP R/3 FOR EVERYONE

STEP-BY-STEP INSTRUCTIONS, PRACTICAL ADVICE, AND
OTHER TIPS AND TRICKS FOR WORKING WITH SAP

Jim Mazzullo
Peter Wheatley

**Prentice Hall Professional
Technical Reference**

Upper Saddle River, NJ • Boston • Indianapolis • San Francisco
New York • Toronto • Montreal • London • Munich • Paris • Madrid
Capetown • Sydney • Tokyo • Singapore • Mexico City

Many of the designations used by manufacturers and sellers to distinguish their products are claimed as trademarks. Where those designations appear in this book, and the publisher was aware of a trademark claim, the designations have been printed with initial capital letters or in all capitals.

The authors and publisher have taken care in the preparation of this book, but make no expressed or implied warranty of any kind and assume no responsibility for errors or omissions. No liability is assumed for incidental or consequential damages in connection with or arising out of the use of the information or programs contained herein.

The publisher offers excellent discounts on this book when ordered in quantity for bulk purchases or special sales, which may include electronic versions and/or custom covers and content particular to your business, training goals, marketing focus, and branding interests. For more information, please contact:

U. S. Corporate and Government Sales
(800) 382-3419
corpsales@pearsontechgroup.com

For sales outside the U. S., please contact:

International Sales
international@pearsoned.com

Visit us on the Web: www.phptr.com

This Book Is Safari Enabled

The Safari® Enabled icon on the cover of your favorite technology book means the book is available through Safari Bookshelf. When you buy this book, you get free access to the online edition for 45 days.

Safari Bookshelf is an electronic reference library that lets you easily search thousands of technical books, find code samples, download chapters, and access technical information whenever and wherever you need it.

To gain 45-day Safari Enabled access to this book:

- Go to http://www.awprofessional.com/safarienabled
- Complete the brief registration form
- Enter the coupon code REET-IQNG-8S9A-SWFE-79BR

If you have difficulty registering on Safari Bookshelf or accessing the online edition, please e-mail customer-service@safaribooksonline.com.

Library of Congress Cataloging-in-Publication Data

Mazzullo, Jim.
    SAP R/3 for everyone : step-by-step instructions, practical advice, and other tips and tricks for working with SAP / Jim Mazzullo, Peter Wheatley.
        p. cm.
    Includes index.
    ISBN 0-13-186085-2 (pbk. : alk. paper)
  1. SAP R/3. 2. Business--Computer programs. 3. Client/server computing. I. Wheatley, Peter. II. Title.
    HF5548.4.R2M39 2005
    658'.05'57585—dc22

                                        2005007985

ISBN 0-13-186085-2
Text printed in the United States on recycled paper at RR Donnelley in Crawfordsville, Indiana.
Second printing, February 2006

CONTENTS

Part IV Working With Output Reports 169

ACKNOWLEDGMENTS

The authors would like to gratefully acknowledge SAP for its kind permission to use its name and trademark, the name of its software product, SAP R/3, and screen images from that product, in this book. We should note that SAP AG is not the publisher of this book and is not responsible for its content in any way.

We would also like to thank our editor, Jill Harry, for her support of this project, and her assistant, Brenda Mulligan, for her support of our efforts. In addition, we would like to thank all the people at Pearson Education Publishing and Addison-Wesley/Prentice Hall for their efforts in producing this book, including Jim Markham, Ebony Haight, Karen Gettman, and Lara Wysong. Finally, we thank our copy editor, Mary Lou Nohr, for her patient and diligent review of our manuscript.

Jim Mazzullo: I would like to acknowledge the support and encouragement of my better half, Maria Landau, who patiently endured my long, and sometimes cranky, days and nights at the computer while I was writing this book. I would also like to acknowledge the help of my good friend and former colleague, Bob Meyer. In addition to his great skills as an SAP functional expert, Bob is an outstanding and patient teacher, and he taught me much of what I know about SAP—but not necessarily everything *he* knows. Bob did not contribute any content to this book, but the confident and practical approach that it takes to SAP was entirely inherited from him.

Peter Wheatley: I would like to acknowledge my mother, father, and brother for their unwavering support and lifelong guidance. I would also like to acknowledge my loving wife, Ana, for her unearthly patience, understanding, and strength, and my three sons, John, Austin, and Cameron, for their childlike wonder, energy, and love. Lastly, I would be remiss if I did not acknowledge my friends at SAP for their support, advice, and true friendship.

ABOUT THE AUTHORS

Jim Mazzullo was born and raised in Brooklyn, New York, the son of Joseph and Mary Mazzullo, who operated a small luncheonette on Bath Avenue. He is a graduate of Brooklyn College, where he earned his bachelor's degree in geology in 1977, and the University of South Carolina, where he earned his doctorate in that same field in 1981.

Jim began his professional career as a research professor and an instructor of geology at Texas A&M University, then worked for a large electric utility company in Portland, Oregon, where he developed, coordinated, and delivered training in SAP and other system and desktop applications.

Jim is now a consulting scientific and technical trainer, curriculum developer, and writer. He lives in Portland with his better half Maria, and their two very spoiled cats, Smokey and Deva. You can learn more about him on his Web site: www.JimMazzullo.com

Peter Wheatley was born in Frankfurt, Germany, the son of career military officer CW4 John (Ret.) and Jean Wheatley. He is a 1993 graduate of the University of Texas at El Paso in management information systems and finance. He also completed his master's degree in business administration at the University of Texas at El Paso in 1995.

Peter began his professional career as a developer for IBM, then continued as an SAP developer and production planning analyst at Compaq. Peter has spent the last seven years employed at SAP America in several roles: consultant, technical consultant manager, and technical solutions architect.

Peter currently oversees SAP implementations as a customer engagement manager in the Southwest region of SAP America. He lives in Houston with his wife, Ana, and their three wonderful sons, John, Austin, and Cameron.

PREFACE

Welcome to the world of SAP! You are now embarking on a journey into the workings and use of SAP R/3, the leading business enterprise software in the world.[1]

This book is written for the nontechnical end user of SAP R/3; that is, an average person in a company who has perhaps had some experience with desktop applications like *MS Word* and *Excel* but little or no experience with more complex enterprise software. This book provides these users with detailed instructions for working with this outstanding and versatile software product.

These instructions do not address any specific purpose, such as working with budget and cost data or managing the inventory of a warehouse. Rather, they describe general or *universal* procedures for working with any part of the software for any purpose. We firmly believe that a solid grasp of these general procedures and the development of the skills for executing them are the real secret for learning and managing SAP R/3 and using it effectively at your job.

In addition, this book is not intended to be comprehensive. SAP R/3 is very complex in its design and operation, and a comprehensive description of this software would require a much larger—not to mention more expensive—"bible" of a book that most people could not lift. Rather, this book describes the techniques and procedures that are most frequently employed by nontechnical end users when they work with SAP R/3. We decided on its contents after years of using this software, after consulting with other experienced users (the so-called *superusers*) like ourselves, and after many hours in the classroom teaching it to people like you.

Finally, this book is not intended to be a technical treatise about SAP R/3. If you were looking for instructions about programming, developing, or implementing

---

1. SAP stands for *Systems, Applications and Products in Data Processing*; R/3 stands for *Runtime System 3*—in other words, the third release of the software.

the software at your workplace, you bought the wrong book. We do not describe the inner workings or architecture of the SAP software (except very briefly in the following pages), because we have found that such information does not help the typical end user work with the software any more effectively. We also avoid the use of technical jargon throughout this book, and instead say our piece in plain, simple English. We do not use a 25-cent word when a 5-cent word will do.

Before we describe the contents of this book, we must devote some words to the origin, design, and operation of SAP R/3.

What Is SAP R/3?

SAP R/3 is a package of integrated applications called **modules** that record and track the activities and costs of doing business. Its roots extend back to 1972, when five system analysts, all former employees of IBM in Germany, created the software for collecting large volumes of business data in a single computer and then processing this data in *real time*, when the user needs it. Real-time processing was a particularly novel development at the time because the computers of the 1970s were slow, lumbering machines that required minutes, and sometimes even hours, to process large volumes of data.

Since that time, SAP has grown from a small regional company to the leading provider of business enterprise software in the world. At last count, SAP R/3 is now installed at 84,000 locations in 120 countries around the world, and it is used by more than 10 million people every day. SAP is now the world's third-largest independent software vendor, and it is still growing strong.

The great strength and utility of SAP R/3 are due to a large degree to its *architecture* or structure, which consists of **functional modules**, the **SAP database**, and the **graphical user interface** or GUI[2] (Figure P.1). We use the term *system* throughout this book to describe this three-part assemblage of software.

The functional modules are discrete software packages that are dedicated to specific tasks, such as accounting, payroll management, and inventory control (Table P.1). They are typically installed in **application servers**, which are computers that are capable of rapidly processing or "crunching" large volumes of data and then assembling the output of their work in a format that can be read by the user.

---

2. Pronounced "gooey."

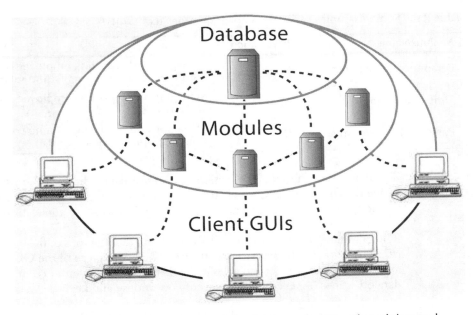

Figure P.1   The SAP R/3 architecture of the database, functional modules, and client graphical user interfaces (GUIs) and their respective hardware components. The modules are all connected to one another, as well as to the database server and the clients.

Table P.1   Some examples of SAP functional modules

Module Name	Abbreviation	Function
Sales and Distribution	SD	Managing and reporting product prices, orders, and delivery, and analyzing production and profit data
Project System	PS	Managing and reporting all phases of a project, including costs, design, approval, and resources
Materials Management	MM	Managing and reporting purchasing, warehousing, and inventorying of goods and materials
Plant Maintenance	PM	Managing and reporting maintenance; inspection and servicing of plants and equipment
Financial Accounting	FI	Managing and reporting corporate cost accounting and budget planning
Controlling	CO	Managing and reporting internal department costs and budgets

Continued

Table P.1   Some examples of SAP functional modules (*continued*)

Module Name	Abbreviation	Function
Personnel Management	PM	Managing and reporting employee data, recruitment, travel, benefits, and salaries
Time Management	TM	Managing and reporting employee time data and payrolls
Personnel Development	PD	Managing and reporting training courses, seminars, and business events

The database is the actual collection of business data. These data are stored inside **database servers**, which are computers with huge amounts of storage memory and the capacity to rapidly exchange data with the application servers.

The graphical user interface or *GUI* appears on the desktops of the computers or *clients* that you use to access the software. The centerpiece of the GUI is the **application window** (called a *session* by SAP), where you enter commands and data on scenes or **screens** by means of your mouse and keyboard.

Note: Some users may access the SAP software through Web browsers such as *MS Internet Explorer*. In these cases, the SAP GUI appears inside the frame of the browser window.

There are many modules in the complete version of SAP R/3, but most business enterprises do not use all of them. Rather, they purchase and install or *implement* only those modules that they need to do their business. The selected modules are then *integrated* or linked to one another and to the database servers and clients by programmers, and the screens are customized or *configured* to fit the enterprise's needs. Once the modules are integrated, the boundaries between them vanish and they work with one another as a single, seamless software package. This aggregation of modules is also very flexible: The enterprise can often add more modules whenever they want so that the software grows as their business needs grow.

SAP Transactions

The word **transaction** describes a single business activity that is conducted with SAP R/3. Some examples of end user transactions are

- Creating a purchase requisition
- Generating a budget report for a company department

- Scheduling the shipment of a material to a plant
- Recording the activities of a maintenance job
- Entering employees' weekly work hours
- Displaying the yearly sales for a product

Every transaction progresses through a four-step **workflow** of actions, commands, and events (Figure P.2).

The typical workflow begins when the end user logs on the SAP system (Step 1). This action calls up the **SAP Easy Access screen**, which is the default "home page" for the software. The end user works with the elements on this screen to call up or *navigate to* the **initial screen** of a transaction (Step 2), where they instruct the software on its specific objectives and then execute it (Step 3). A few seconds later, the output of the transaction appears (Step 4) in one of two forms:

- A confirmation that some business process, such as the creation of a requisition or the entry of an employee's work hours into the database, was accomplished. This message appears by default at the bottom of the initial screen.
- A display of data from the database. This usually appears on its own **output screen**.

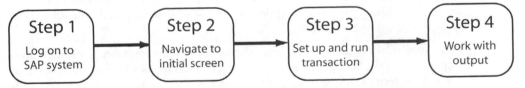

Figure P.2   The SAP workflow. The four parts of this book each cover one step in this process.

A good bit of the communication between the SAP R/3 software and the end user is accomplished during Steps 3 and 4 of this SAP workflow via **technical object codes**.

A technical object is anything that is monitored and tracked by SAP R/3. This includes tangible objects, such as employees, consumable materials, equipment, and physical plants, and intangible ones, such as work orders, purchase requisitions, and shipping orders.

Every technical object has a unique object code, which is assigned to it when its specifications are entered in the SAP database and which is the primary shorthand means of identifying it. There are literally thousands of such codes in every SAP database, but, fortunately, the software provides a way to search for them, so you do not have to memorize or record them.

Organization and Contents of This Book

The body of this book consists of 17 lessons on the general use of SAP R/3. They are grouped into four parts, which correspond to the SAP workflow.

- Part I, *Getting Started*, describes the procedures for logging on and off the SAP R/3 software, customizing the SAP application window and screens to suit your preferences, entering personal and logistical data about yourself, setting default values for the use of the software, and managing your password.

- Part II, *Navigating Between Screens*, describes three methods for navigating from the **SAP Easy Access screen** to the initial screens of transactions, and a fourth method for navigating between initial and output screens.

- Part III, *Setting Up Initial Screens*, describes the procedures for entering and searching for object codes and creating customized versions of initial screens.

- Part IV, *Working With Output Reports*, describes the procedures for customizing the output reports of certain transactions and e-mailing them to other SAP users.

These lessons are preceded by the *Introduction*, which describes the design and operation of the SAP application window and its screens, and followed by a *Coda*, which presents a simple model of the four basic transaction types that are commonly executed by end users.

The instructions in the lessons of this book were written around and illustrated with screens from version 4.7 of the SAP R/3 software. However, they can also be applied to SAP 4.5 and 4.6, which are very similar in their design and operation to SAP 4.7. And with a little effort, they can also be applied to SAP 4.0, which differs slightly in its screen design but not its operation.

Some Words About the Text and Screen Images

This book uses two conventions for highlighting certain texts:

- The names of all screens and screen elements, including all menus, buttons, and fields, are always presented in **bold type**.

- The names of transactions and software, as well as commands, options, and slang terms, are always presented in *italic type*.

These conventions are intended to help the reader scan through the instructions and easily pick out the critical references within them. The bold text can also be found with page references in the index at the back of this book.

In addition, we hereafter refer to the SAP R/3 software simply as *SAP*, and to people who work behind the scenes to install, configure, operate, and monitor the use of the software as the *SAP administrators*.

Finally, we should point out that you will often see small differences between the screen images in this book and your versions of the same screens.

Some of these differences arise because our screens are customized in a slightly different way from your screens. For example, every business enterprise makes use of a unique group of modules in their system, and so they display their own unique set of folders on their **SAP Easy Access screen**. We are no exception to that rule. In addition, we have the most current versions of screens at our disposal, and they contain a few more or different elements, more "bells and whistles," than your screens.

In addition, we have altered many screen images in this book with *Adobe Photoshop* and other tools. For instance, we have routinely cropped nearly all images to fit them on the pages and not consume too much space—otherwise, this book would probably be twice its present length, weight, and price! In addition, we have hidden screen elements and data that are either proprietary in nature or distracting and not relevant to the points of the lessons.

However, these are differences of degree, not of kind. For the most part, you will not even notice the differences between our screens and your screens, and the noticeable differences will neither confuse you nor obscure the lessons in this book.

Introduction

DESIGN AND OPERATION OF THE SAP APPLICATION WINDOW

We begin this book with a visual tour of the SAP **application window**[1] and a discussion of the design and operation of its **screen elements**.

When you launch SAP, a *session* or an application window appears on your computer desktop with a display of a scene or **screen** inside its frame. This screen changes in its appearance and function as you progress through the SAP workflow from the **SAP Easy Access screen** (the default "home page" of the system) to the initial screen of a transaction (where you set up and execute it) and finally to the output for that transaction.

Regardless of their function, however, seven features or **elements** are found on every screen of the SAP application window (Figure I.1):

- Menu bar (A)
- Standard toolbar (B)
- Title bar (C)
- Application toolbar (D)
- Central work area (E)
- Status bar (F)
- Popup screens (not shown here)

This lesson describes the design and operation of these screen elements—all of which should be familiar to the reader, by the way, as they can also be found in the application windows of many common desktop software applications, such as

---

1. SAP uses the term *session* to describe the frame of its screens, but we use the more familiar term *application window* throughout this book.

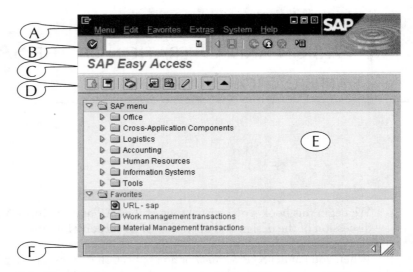

Figure I.1   The **SAP Easy Access screen** contains all the elements found on other screens in the system.

MS Word and *Excel.* We use the **SAP Easy Access screen** as the principal source of our screen images in this introduction because it contains all these screen elements and should be familiar to even the novice users of the system, but we also present images from other SAP screens to bring some variety to this discussion.

Incidentally, this introduction focuses on the design and operation of the SAP application window as it appears in the desktop GUI. However, some end users access SAP through Web browsers such as *MS Internet Explorer,* where the SAP application window is condensed into a simpler format. We describe and illustrate this condensed design at the end of this introduction.

Menu Bar

The **menu bar** is the uppermost element on all screens. It contains three components (Figure I.2):

- **Menu headers** (A)
- **System shortcut menu icon** (B)
- **Control buttons** (C)

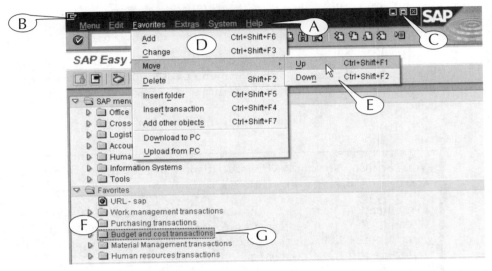

Figure I.2   The menu bar and its components, with a display of the **Favorites menu** and one of its submenus.

Menu Headers

When the menu headers are clicked, they display lists or **menus** (D) of nearly every command that can be executed on a screen. Some of the commands in the menus have their own **submenus** (E), which are displayed when your cursor lands on those commands. The presence of such submenus is indicated by arrows to the far right of the commands.

To execute a command from the menu bar with your mouse:

- Click a header to display its menu.

- Scroll down and across the menu and submenus to the desired command. Notice that each command is highlighted when your cursor lands on it.

- When you reach the desired command, click your mouse again to select it.

For example, the **SAP Easy Access screen** contains a set of folders called the **Favorites** (F), in which you can store links to the initial screens of frequently run transactions (see Lesson 6). You can shift the *Budget and cost transactions folder* (G) upwards through the list of these folders by doing the following:

- Click the folder to select and highlight it (G).

- Click the **Favorites header** to display its menu (D).

- Scroll down to the *Move command*, then slide over to the *Up command* and click it.

This sequence of actions is called the **menu path** for that command. It is presented throughout this book in this format:

Favorites > Move > Up

You can also use your keyboard to display and select commands from the menu bar, if you are so inclined.

Every header in a menu bar has one underlined letter in its name. For instance, the **Menu header** of the **SAP Easy Access screen** has an underlined *M*, the **Edit header** has an underlined *E* and so on (Figure I.2). This letter identifies the **display key** for that header.

You can display a menu by pressing and holding the **Alt key** on your keyboard and then hitting its display key. Once the menu appears, use the arrow keys to move up, down, left, or right through the menu and submenus to the desired command, then hit the **Enter key** on your keyboard to select it.

Menu bars are generally *screen specific;* that is, they change with the scene inside the application window. For an example, let us compare the menu bars of the **SAP Easy Access screen** (Figure I.2) and the output screen of the *IE03 transaction* (Figure I.3).

The **SAP Easy Access screen** appears when you log on to the system and is the starting point in the SAP workflow. From here, you move or *navigate* to the initial screen of a transaction, where you set it up and execute it. Consequently, the first four menus in its menu bar—*Menu*, *Edit*, *Favorites*, and *Extras*—contain commands for customizing the screen for easier navigation. For example, the **Favorites menu** (D) contains all sorts of commands for working with the **Favorites folders**, where links to your frequently run transactions are stored (see Lesson 6).

In contrast, the output screen of the *IE03 transaction* displays data about a piece of equipment. Consequently, the first six menus in its menu bar—*Equipment*, *Edit*, *Goto*, *Extras*, *Structure*, and *Environment*—contain commands for working with such data. For example, the **Environment menu** (Figure I.3A) contains commands such as *Orders*, which displays a list of all the maintenance work done

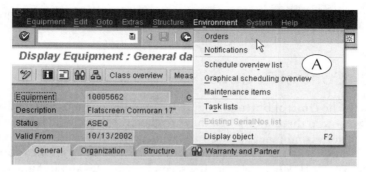

Figure I.3   The menu bar of the output screen of the *IE03 transactions* contains headers that are appropriate to equipment displays.

on the equipment; *Notifications*, which displays a list of all maintenance requests for it; and *Schedule overview list*, which displays its maintenance schedule.

However, the menu bar of every screen contains the **System** and **Help menus** at its right end. The first menu contains commands for opening, closing, and customizing the SAP application window, printing screens, logging off, and other system-related processes, and the second gives you access to the help features of the system. We describe some of the commands of these two menus in the lessons of Part I of this book.

System Shortcut Menu Icon

When it is clicked, the **system shortcut menu icon** displays a short menu of commands (Figure I.4A) for working with the SAP application window. Most of these commands can also be executed by the **System menu** of the menu bar and by other, more convenient, means. The single exception is the *Stop transaction command*, which kills a transaction after you start its execution.

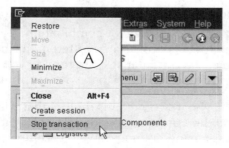

Figure I.4   The system shortcut menu.

We describe the system shortcut menu and its functions in more detail in Lesson 2 of this book.

Control Buttons

The **control buttons** (Figure I.2C) of the menu bar affect the application window in three ways when they are clicked. (You should be familiar with their functions from other applications, which often have these same buttons in the same location.) The first reduces the window to a small **application bar** at the bottom of the *Windows* desktop; the second maximizes and minimizes its size; and the third closes it.

We describe and illustrate the uses of the control buttons in more detail in Lesson 2 of this book.

You can use your mouse in four ways on the screen elements of the SAP application window: You can *click, right-click, double-click*, and *click-and-drag*.

- When you are instructed to *click* a screen element, move your cursor atop that element and then quickly click and release the *left button* on your mouse.
- When you are instructed to *right-click* a screen element, move your cursor atop that element and quickly click and release the *right button* on your mouse.
- When you are instructed to *double-click* a screen element, move your cursor atop that element and quickly click and release the *left button* on your mouse *twice*.
- When you are instructed to *click-and-drag* a screen element, move your cursor atop that element; click *and hold down* the *left button* on your mouse; slide the cursor across the screen to its destination, then release the left button.

You can also use single or combination keystrokes to execute certain commands. Keystrokes are written in this book in bold letters (for example, "hit the **Enter key**") to remind you that the action takes place on your keyboard rather than your monitor.

Some keyboard commands require that you press and hold down one key and then press a second key. For example, you can print a screen by pressing and holding down the **Control** (**Ctrl**) **key** and then pressing the **P key** on your keyboard. This particular command is presented in the format **Ctrl + P** in this book.

Standard Toolbar

The **standard toolbar** (Figure I.5) contains the **command field** and several **command buttons** for working on screens and navigating between them. The name of this toolbar comes from the fact that the functions of these components are commonly executed on, or *universal* to, every screen, regardless of its specific purpose. Consequently, this toolbar is found on every screen in the SAP application.

Figure I.5   Components of the standard toolbar

Command Field

The **command field** is another tool for navigating to the initial screens of transactions. Every initial screen in the SAP application is identified by a unique **transaction code**. You can navigate to that screen by entering that code in this field.

The **command field** also contains a **list icon** at its right end (Figure I.6A). This feature, which is found inside other fields on many screens, displays a list of recently entered transaction codes (B) when it is clicked.

Lastly, the **command field** is accompanied by its own control arrow (C), which displays or hides the field when it is clicked. (We recommend that you keep this field open at all times so that you can use it for navigation.)

We describe the use of the **command field** in more detail in Lesson 7 of this book.

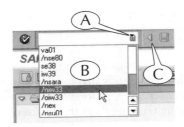

Figure I.6   The history button (A) of the **Command field** reveals a list of recently used transaction codes (B).

Command Buttons

The **command buttons** execute universal tasks, such as entering and saving data, printing a screen, and navigating back to the previous screen, when they are clicked. You can display a label that describes the function of a button by placing your cursor over it (Figure I.7). If the command can also be executed from your keyboard, the keystroke will also be displayed in parentheses in the label.

Figure I.7   Place your cursor over a button to see a label with its description and an alternative keystroke for that command (in this case, the **F3 function button**).

Here are some of the important design and operation features of the standard toolbar.

1. You can vary the width of the application window with the frame grabber in its lower-right corner (see Lesson 2). But if the window is too narrow, the buttons on the right end of the standard toolbar are cut off and replaced by a **list button** (Figure I.8A). However, you can click this button to display a menu of the hidden commands (B), then scroll down and click one to execute it.

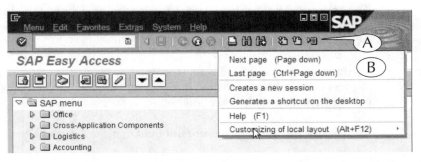

Figure I.8   You can display the hidden commands of a shortened standard toolbar by clicking the list button (A).

2. Some of the buttons in the standard toolbar provide convenient shortcuts for commands that can be executed from the menu bar. For example, the **Create session** and **Create shortcut buttons** are shortcuts for the same commands in the **System menu**.

3. Some of the functions of the buttons can also be executed with key-strokes. For example, you can print a screen's content either by clicking the **Print button** in the standard toolbar or by the keystroke **Ctrl + P**.

Similarly, you can enter data on a screen by clicking the **Enter button** in the standard toolbar or by hitting the **Enter key** on your keyboard. We always instruct you to use the keyboard for this command because it is faster.

4. On any given screen, some of the buttons in the standard toolbar appear in full color and others are "grayed out." The full-colored buttons are active or *hot*—that is, they function on that screen—while the gray ones are inactive or *cold* because they serve no purpose there.

For example, the **Save, Back,** and **Cancel buttons** are all grayed out on the **SAP Easy Access screen** because there is nothing to save, no screen to return to (this is the "home page"), and nothing to cancel (Figure I.1).

Title Bar

The **title bar** displays the name of the screen in the application window. The title bars of initial screens usually indicate the transaction type (see the *Coda* for a discussion of transaction types) and the object of the transaction (Figure I.9A), while the title bars of output screens usually display these same data along with the code for the object of the transaction (Figure I.9B).

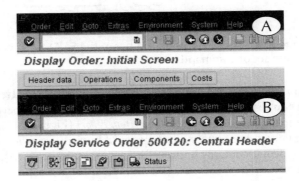

Figure I.9   Some examples of the title bars of initial (A) and output screens (B).

In this book, we refer to all screens by the name in their title bars, printed in bold letters. When we refer to the name of an output screen, we replace the specific object code with a general reference. For example, we would present the title of the screen in Figure I.9B as **Display Service Order [Order Number]: Central Header.**

Application Toolbar

The **application toolbar** contains a second row of command buttons for executing certain tasks. Like the standard toolbar, the buttons of the application toolbar replicate commands in the menu bar. In addition, you can display a label that describes the function of any button by placing your cursor over it. But unlike the standard toolbar, the buttons of the application toolbar change from screen to screen—that is, they change with the *application* or function of the screen.

For instance, the central work area of the **SAP Easy Access screen** (Figure I.1E) displays the **SAP User** and **Favorites folders**, which contain links for moving to the initial screens of transactions as well as the **Business Workplace screen**. The application toolbar of this screen contains eight buttons for issuing commands that are related to these screen elements (Figure I.10).

- The first two buttons (A) display different versions of the folder sets in the central work area (see Lesson 5).

- The third button (B) calls up the **Business Workplace screen** (see Lesson 17).

- The last five buttons (C) enable you to create and manage the **Favorites folders** of the central work area (see Lesson 6).

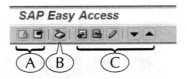

Figure I.10   The application toolbar of the **SAP Easy Access screen** has its own unique set of command buttons.

On the other hand, the **Display Actual Costs Line Items for Cost Centers screen** displays data about the expenditures for a department (or *cost center*) in a company in a multicolumn *line-item report* (Figure I.11). Its application toolbar contains a completely different set of buttons for working with this report. For instance, it contains buttons for sorting its contents (A), summing up the numerical values in its columns (B), and e-mailing the report to another SAP user (C).

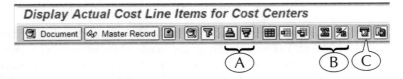

Figure I.11   The application toolbar of the **Display Actual Costs Line Items for Cost Centers screen** has its own unique set of command buttons.

Status Bar

The **status bar** (Figure I.12) contains three components: the **message field** (A), **system data field** (B), and **frame grabber** (C).

The message field is one of two screen elements (the second is **popup screens**) by which the system displays confirmations, warnings, errors, and other messages to users. For example:

- When you set up and execute a transaction for creating a requisition, the system confirms you have successfully completed the transaction and displays by default the new requisition number in the message field (Figure I.12A). You don't have to respond to the system in any way, although you should probably record the requisition number.

- If you try to log on with the wrong user ID or password, the system displays an error message to this effect in the message field. Once again, you do not have to respond directly to this message, but you must correct your error when you try to log on again. You can also see more information about a warning or an error by double-clicking the message.

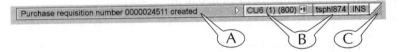

Figure I.12 Components of the status bar.

The **system data field** displays technical data about your SAP environment; that is, its hardware and software. Some of these data appear directly on the status bar. For example, the system data field in Figure I.12 displays the name of the database (*CU6 (1) (800)*) that we used to capture the screen images for this book, and the server (*tsphl874*) through which we accessed this database (B).

You can also click the **list icon** (Figure I.13A) in the **system data field** to display other sorts of technical data, including the name of the database (*System*) and SAP server (*Host name*), your user ID (*User*), and the transaction code of the screen (*Transaction*). You can permanently display one of these datatypes directly in the first compartment of the status bar by scrolling down to it and clicking it so that a check appears to the left of its name (B).

Finally, you can display or hide the **system data field** by clicking the control arrow (Figure I.13C) to its left.

The **frame grabber** (Figure I.12C) allows you to adjust the size and shape of the application window by clicking-and-dragging it into a new position.

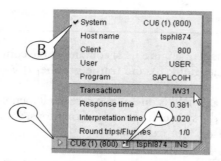

Figure I.13   The list menu icon (A) reveals other technical data about SAP.

Central Work Area

The **central work area** (technically called the *Dynpro*) lies between the application toolbar and status bar of every screen. This is the principal working environment for the SAP application. It contains many different screen elements for navigating between screens, setting up transactions, and working with their output. We describe the design and operation of these screen elements in the remaining pages of this introduction.

Panels and Panes

The central work area can contain one or more **panels**. Single-panel work areas are most common, but two- and three-panel work areas can also be found on the **SAP Easy Access screen** and some initial and output screens (Figure I.14). Wherever you find multiple panels, you can adjust their sizes by clicking-and-dragging the dividers or **panes** between them (Figure I.14A).

Some multipanel screens have buttons in their main application toolbars (or in secondary toolbars above the panels themselves) for displaying and hiding panels. For example, the initial screen for the *Create Purchase Order transaction* (Figure I.14) has a side panel that can be used for searching for older requisitions. You can hide this panel, which is not required for running the transaction, by clicking the **Document overview off button**[2] (B) in the main application toolbar of the screen. When this panel is hidden, this button changes into the **Document overview on button** (Figure I.15A), which can be used to display the panel.

---

2. This button goes by other names, such as **Navigation on/off** and **Close/Open**, on other screens.

hidden, and the **Close button** (B), which hides an area when it is displayed. We have displayed the line-item table and hidden the *Header* and *Item* subscreens above and below it (so that only their names appear) by these means in our example.

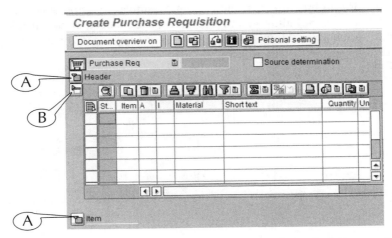

Figure I.19   The Expand (A) and Close (B) buttons display and hide (respectively) parts of the central work area. In this image, the *Header* and *Item* subscreens are both hidden, and only their names appear.

Selection Boxes, Check Boxes, and Radio Buttons

Selection boxes (Figure I.20) and **check boxes** (Figure I.21) are found on the initial and output screens of many transactions, where they can be used to select *one or more* options, objects, or commands from a roster of items. You can select and deselect items in these rosters by clicking these boxes.

The difference between selection boxes and check boxes is simply the result of clicking them. When you click a selection box, it highlights the name of the selected item (Figure I.20A); when you click a check box, a check appears inside it.

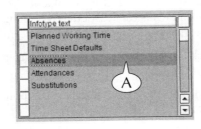

Figure I.20   When a selection box is clicked, the name of the selected item is highlighted (A).

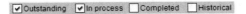

Figure I.21   Check boxes.

Radio buttons (Figure I.22) serve a similar function to selection and check boxes: they allow you to select an option, object, or command from a roster of such items. However, they differ in one key regard: you can only select *one* item from the roster with a radio button.

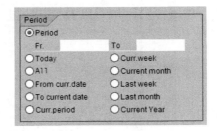

Figure I.22   Radio buttons.

Command Buttons

Command buttons can often be found in the central work areas of screens (see Figure I.17G). Like the buttons of the standard and application toolbars, they execute a specific task, which you can identify by placing your cursor over them to display their label.

Scroll Bars

Scroll bars appear along the bottom and right margin of especially long or wide screens. You use them to shift the scene in the central work area in the horizontal or vertical direction (Figure I.23) in one of three ways.

1. Click the arrows at the end of a bar (A) to move the scene in small increments. This is the least effective and most tedious method, because the scene "creeps" slowly through the central work area.

2. Click the blue stripe of the bar (B) to move the scene in large increments.

3. Click-and-drag the white bar (C) to move the scene by any distance.

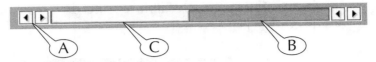

Figure I.23   Scroll bar.

You can also use the four **page control buttons** in the standard toolbar (Figure I.5 on page 7) to shift the scene in a long central work area in the vertical direction.

The first and last buttons, which have a design of double arrows over a page icon, shift the scene to the very top and very bottom, respectively, of the central work area. The two middle buttons, which have single arrows imposed over a page icon, shift the scene to the next full scene above and below the present one.

Popup Screens

Popup screens (also known as *dialog boxes*) of all different sizes are often displayed within SAP application windows. Some appear in response to an action by you or a command from you to the system, and others appear automatically when the system wants to communicate information to you.

Popup screens can be *informational, interrogatory,* or *procedural* in their purpose.

Informational popup screens (Figure I.24) display a message from the system and require only that you acknowledge that message by clicking an **Enter button** (which usually appears at its bottom) or hitting the **Enter key** on your keyboard. Such popup screens are generally small, given their limited function, and they appear without a specific command on your part.

Figure I.24   An informational popup screen.

Interrogatory popup screens (Figure I.25) display questions from the system in response to some action on your part and require some response from you. For example, when you try to log off the system (see Lesson 1), the system displays a popup screen that asks you to confirm or cancel that action with the **Yes** and **No buttons**. Such popup screens are also generally small.

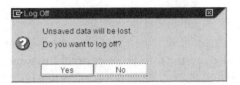

Figure I.25   A query popup screen.

Procedural popup screens allow you to conduct certain procedures outside the central work area of screens. For example, you can control the display in the central work area of the **SAP Easy Access screen** with a procedural popup screen (Figure I.26), which you can call up by following the menu path **Extras > Settings** on that screen. Procedural popup screens are medium to large in size and fairly complex in their composition, often containing their own toolbar (which usually runs along their bottoms), tabbed subscreens, and other screen elements.

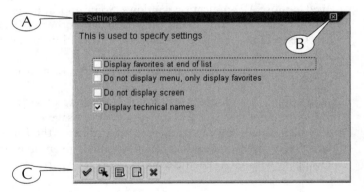

Figure I.26   A procedural popup screen.

The name of a popup screen is always displayed in a blue **title bar** across its top (Figure I-26A). This bar also contains a control button at its right end (B) that you can click to erase the screen. You will also find a button for this purpose, along with other command buttons, in a toolbar at the bottom of a procedural popup screen (C).

SAP on the Web

Many end users access the SAP system through an application window that is displayed directly on their computer monitor's desktop, or what is called the *client server GUI*. However, it is also possible to access the system through a Web browser such as *MS Internet Explorer*.

When you access SAP through a Web browser, the SAP application window appears within the frame of the browser's application window (Figure I-27). For the most part, the design and operation of this *Web GUI* are identical to the design and operation of the desktop window, except in *one* regard: the menu bar and standard toolbar are collapsed onto the application toolbar, where they are represented by buttons.

For example, Figure I-27 shows the design of the **SAP Easy Access screen** within the Web browser window. This screen contains only the title bar and application toolbar at its top; its menu bar and standard toolbar are replaced by

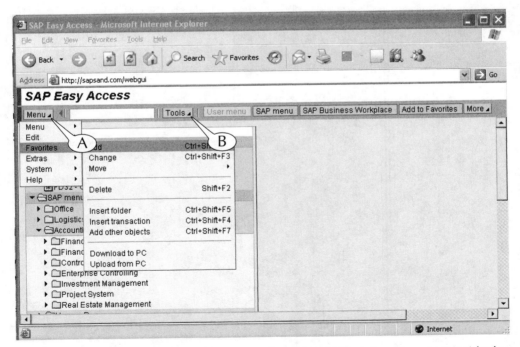

Figure I.27   The SAP application window is condensed in design when it appears inside the frame of a Web browser window: Its menu bar and standard toolbar are collapsed onto its application toolbar. Click the **Menu button** to reveal the menu headers. The commands of the Favorites menu are shown in this image.

the **Menu button** (A) and **Tool button** (B), which are situated on the application toolbar. You need only click the **Menu button** to display and maneuver to all its familiar command menus and submenus, and click the **Tool button** to display and select from its commands.

Part I
GETTING STARTED

"Begin at the beginning," the King said, very gravely, "and go on till you come to the end: then stop." — Lewis Carroll (British author), Alice in Wonderland

Lesson 1: Logging On and Logging Off

Lesson 2: Working With SAP Sessions

Lesson 3: Entering User Profile Data

Lesson 4: Changing Your Password

You can create one or more desktop shortcuts for logging on to the system. (See the instructions in Lesson 4.) Each desktop shortcut has the following convenient features:

- It is rigged to log on to a specific server, so you do not need to select a server with the **SAP Logon pad**.

- It is rigged to know your user ID, client number, and language code, so you do not need to enter these data on the **SAP screen**. Rather, you simply provide your password on a small popup screen.

- It is rigged to display a specific *target screen* once you log on. The **SAP Easy Access screen**, which is the home page of the system, is the usual preferred destination (and the target of the desktop shortcut in Figure 1.4), but you can also create desktop shortcuts that call up other screens when you log on.

Procedure

Logging On With a Desktop Shortcut

Step 1. Double-click the icon for the desktop shortcut (Figure 1.4).

Step 2. The **SAP Easy Access popup screen** appears (Figure 1.5). It contains only the **User Name** and **Password fields**.

- Confirm your user ID in the **User name field** (A).

- Enter your password in the **Password field** (B).

- Hit the **Enter key** on your keyboard.

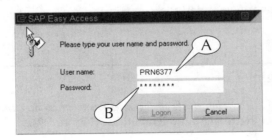

Figure 1.5 The **SAP Easy Access popup screen** allows for quick logons to the system.

Step 3. The SAP application window appears and displays your target screen (the **SAP Easy Access screen**, in this case). You are now ready to work with the system.

End Procedure

The most common problem you will probably encounter during logon is the failure of the system to recognize a code that you might have entered in one of the four fields of the **SAP screen**. When you enter wrong codes, the system responds with a message in the status bar of the screen (Figure 1.6) that something is not correct.

This error is most often due to typing errors. Check that the **Caps Lock key** on your computer keyboard is disengaged, then reenter your codes more carefully.

For security purposes, some SAP administrators program their system to erase the **SAP screen** and freeze you out of the logon process when you fail to log on with the correct codes several times in a row. When this occurs, you must contact your SAP administrator to regain authorization to use the system.

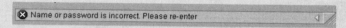

Figure 1.6   The system posts a message in the status bar if you enter the wrong code on the **SAP screen**.

Logging Off

You can log off from any screen in the SAP system. There are three alternative procedures for this action, depending on whether you have one or several open sessions on your desktop.

Procedure

Logging Off

Step 1. *If you have only one open session (application window)*, click the third control button (A) in the menu bar (Figure 1.7).

If you have several open sessions, you can either

▪ Follow the menu path **System > Log off** (B), *or*

Enter */nex* in the **command field**[2] (C), and hit the **Enter key** on your keyboard.

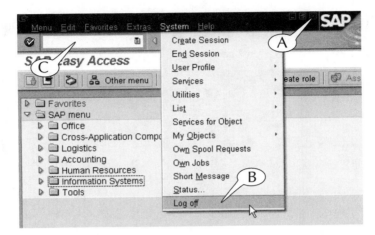

Figure 1.7   You can log off by clicking the third control button, using the **System menu**, or entering */nex* in the **command field**.

Step 2.   The **Log Off screen** appears, and you are asked to confirm the action (Figure 1.8).

- Click the **Yes button**, *or*

  Hit the **Enter key** on your keyboard.

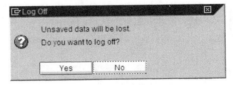

Figure 1.8   Confirm the log-off with this screen by clicking the **Yes button** or hitting the **Enter key** on your keyboard.

End Procedure

---

2. We describe this and other uses of the command field in Lesson 7.

Lesson 2
WORKING WITH SAP SESSIONS

The SAP application window (technically called a *session*) is a **graphical user interface** or *GUI* with which you communicate and interact with the SAP system. This interaction occurs on three types of screens that are displayed within the frame of the application window:

- The **SAP Easy Access screen**, which is the default home page of the system and the starting point for most transactions

- The initial screens of transactions, where you set up and execute transactions

- The output screens of transactions, where the system displays the results of transactions to you

This second lesson provides instructions on managing the properties of the SAP application window and its screens. Six topics are discussed:

- Controlling the session geometry and location

- Creating multiple sessions

- Killing a session

- Customizing the layouts of sessions and screens

- Customizing the **SAP Easy Access screen**

- Creating desktop shortcuts

Controlling the Application Window Geometry and Location

You can change the size, shape and location of the SAP application window with several screen elements.

Killing a Session

Once you set up the initial screen of a transaction and execute it, a small stop-watch (A) appears at the left end of the status bar of that screen and remains there until the transaction is finished (Figure 2.4). During this time, you can cancel the transaction, or *kill the session*, through the **system control menu**.

There are two common situations in which you might decide to cancel a transaction. Both occur during *reporting transactions*, which search through the database for the records of one or more *objects*.[2] (See the *Coda* at the end of this book for a discussion of the basic transaction types.)

The first situation: You are running a *display transaction*, which displays the database record for a single object, but you entered the wrong code for that object. For instance, you may have wanted to display the data record for purchase requisition #123456, but you mistakenly entered the code for purchase requisition #654321 on the initial screen of the transaction.

The second situation: You are running a *list-display transaction*, which displays a list of all objects that are related in some fashion. However, you define the search so broadly that the system must search a large volume of the database, and so the transaction takes a very long time to execute. For instance, you may have wanted to display a list of all the purchase requisitions that you created for your department during the last six months, but you neglected to enter this time period on the initial screen of the transaction. This forces the system to search the database for *every* requisition that you ever created for your department since you started working there.

To kill *any* transaction (reporting *or* process), follow this next procedure.

Procedure

Cancelling a Transaction

Step 1. Click the **system control menu icon** (B) in the upper left-hand corner to display the system control menu (Figure 2.4).

---

2. An object is anything that is assigned a code in SAP.

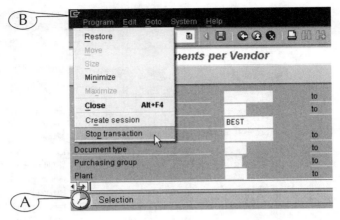

Figure 2.4   You can cancel a transaction with the **system control menu**, which is displayed in the upper-left corner of the application window.

Step 2.   Scroll down to the *Stop transaction command*, and click it to select it.

Step 3.   The transaction is cancelled, and the initial screen of the transaction is replaced by the **SAP Easy Access screen**.

End Procedure

Customizing the Layout of Application Windows and Screens

The design and operation of SAP application windows and screens are, for the most part, firmly established by the designers of the software. However, you can customize a few layout features with the **Customizing of local layout menu**. You can display this menu by clicking the **Customize local layout button** (A), which lies at the right end of the standard toolbar (Figure 2.5).

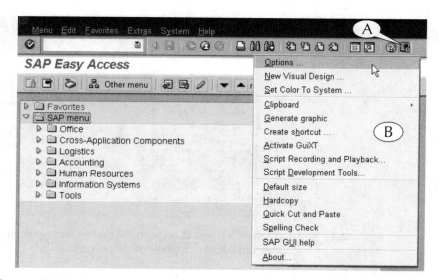

Figure 2.5 The **Customize local layout button** reveals a long menu of commands, including two commands for customizing the design and operation of SAP windows and screens: *Options* and *New Visual Design*.

The **Customizing menu** (Figure 2.5B) contains a long list of commands, many of which do not affect the layouts of application windows and screens. We explore the use of some of these commands in later parts in this book. You may also want to experiment with them to determine their functions on your own.

You can customize the layout with the first two commands in this menu: *Options* and *New Visual Design*. Simply follow the next two procedures.

Procedure

Customizing With the Options Command

Step 1. Click the **Customizing of local layout button** (A) to display its menu, then follow the menu path

   Customizing of local options > Options (Figure 2.5).

Step 2. The **Options popup screen** appears (Figure 2.6). It displays one of six scenes or **subscreens**, which can be selected with the tabs and tab controls (A) at its top. The **Options subscreen** is displayed by default when this screen appears.

   ▪ Select the *Quick option* on the **Options subscreen** (B).

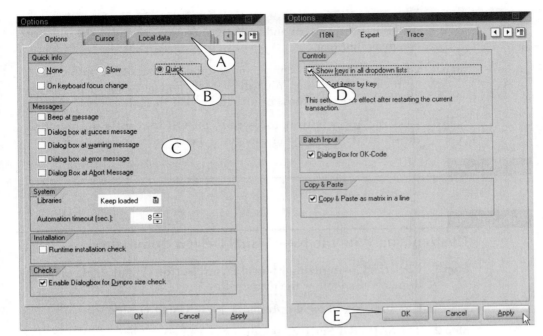

Figure 2.6   The **Options** and **Extras screens** enable you to change some of the layout features of sessions and screens.

Why do this? Whenever your cursor lands on a button on a screen, the system flashes a label that identifies its function. This selection causes that label to appear rapidly.

- *Optional:* Select or deselect the *Beep at message option* in the **Messages field area** (C).

Why do this? The system occasionally sends messages and warnings to you. This option either sets the system to announce such messages with a beep or disables that sound effect. (We chose to disable it because beeps annoy us.)

- *Optional:* Select any or all of the four *Dialog box at [message type] options* in the **Messages field area** (C).

Why do this? SAP usually displays confirmation, warning, error, and abort messages in the **status bar** at the bottom of the screen by default. By selecting these options, the system instead displays such messages in a popup screen in the central work area.

Step 3. Click the **Expert tab**.

- Select the *Show keys in all dropdown lists option* (D).

Why do this? This action displays alternative keystrokes for many commands in the menu bar and toolbars of the screens and in the labels of command buttons.

Step 4. Click the other tabs, examine and test the other available options, and set them to your liking. You will probably find (as we have) that they are either obscure in purpose or set at acceptable default values.

Step 5. Click the **Apply button**, followed by the **OK button**, at the bottom of the screen (E) to save your changes and erase it from your desktop.

End Procedure

Procedure

Customizing With the New Visual Design Command

Step 1. Click the **Customizing of local layout button** (Figure 2.5A) to display its menu, then follow the menu path

Customizing of local options > New Visual Design.

Step 2. The **SAP GUI Settings popup screen** appears (Figure 2.7). It has two tabs (A) at its top for displaying two separate subscreens. The **General tab** is selected by default when the screen appears.

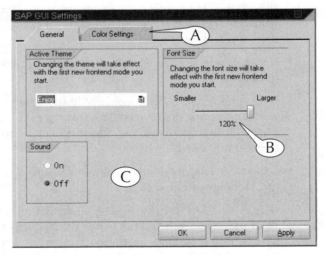

Figure 2.7   You can control font sizes and sound effects with the **General subscreen** of the **SAP GUI Settings screen.**

Procedure

Creating Desktop Shortcuts

Step 1. Navigate to a screen that will be the target of the desktop shortcut. For this example, we create a shortcut to the **SAP Easy Access screen**, which is the most convenient starting point for working with the system.

Step 2. Click the **Create shortcut button** (A) in the standard toolbar of the screen (Figure 2.13).

Figure 2.13   The **Create shortcut button**.

Step 3. The **New SAP GUI Shortcut popup screen** appears (Figure 2.14). It contains several fields that are prepopulated with codes for the server (A), client (B), language (C) and target screen (D) among others. (*Note: Session Manager* is another name for the **SAP Easy Access screen**.)

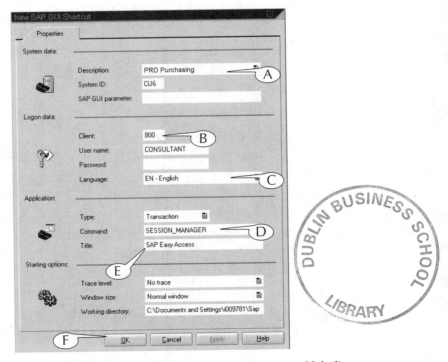

Figure 2.14   The **New SAP GUI Shortcut popup screen** for creating and labeling a desktop shortcut.

- Enter a label for the new icon in the **Title field** (E). This label will appear beneath the icon on your desktop.

Step 4. Click the **Apply button**, followed by the **OK button**, at the bottom of the popup screen (F).

Step 5. A second **SAP GUI Shortcut popup screen** appears to confirm that the desktop shortcut is created (Figure 2.15).

- Hit the **Enter key** on your keyboard to erase this screen. The icon for the new shortcut appears on your desktop.

Figure 2.15 The **SAP GUI Shortcut popup screen** confirms that a shortcut is created.

End Procedure

Lesson 3
ENTERING USER PROFILE DATA

SAP stores a record of personal, organizational, and contact data about you in its database. This record is called your **user profile**, and it includes your name, title, location, and phone numbers, as well as your preferences on dates, number formats, and output printer.

You are responsible for maintaining the data in your user profile. You should enter data there as soon as you begin to use the SAP system, then update it whenever there is some change in these data—for example, when you change work location or get promoted to a new job. It is especially important to keep your location and contact data current, because other users who are trying to locate or communicate with you may call up your SAP user profile for this data.

Procedure

Entering User Profile Data

Step 1. Go to the menu bar at the top of *any* SAP screen and follow the menu path **System > User Profile > Own Data** (Figure 3.1A).

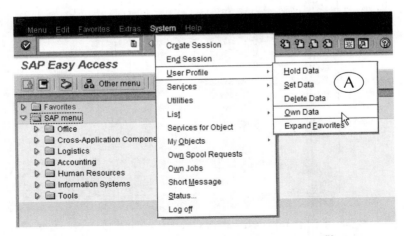

Figure 3.1 The menu path for calling up the **Maintain User Profile screen**.

Step 2. The **Maintain User Profile popup screen** appears (Figure 3.2). It can display three subscreens, which you select with the tabs (A) at its top. You can enter your user profile data on two of its subscreens: **Address** and **Defaults**.

The **Address subscreen** is displayed by default when this screen appears. It contains several fields for entering your personal, logistical, and contact data.

- Enter data in any fields on the **Address subscreen**. For this example, the user entered his title, name, department, location, and telephone number.

Note: Some fields on this screen contain **list icons** (B). Click this icon to reveal a list of possible entries for such a field, then scroll down to and click the desired entry.

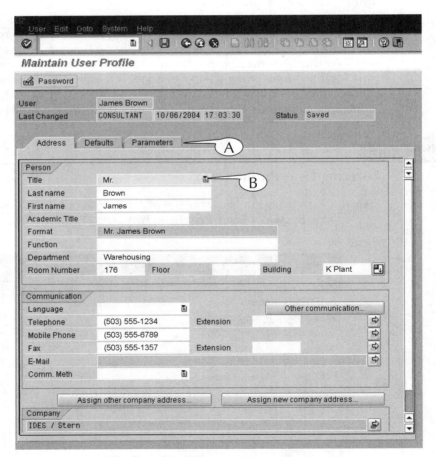

Figure 3.2   Enter personal and logistical data about yourself on the **Address subscreen** of the **Maintain User Profile screen**.

Step 3. Click the **Defaults tab** to display the **Defaults subscreen** (Figure 3.3), where you can enter default values for several functions and formats of the system.

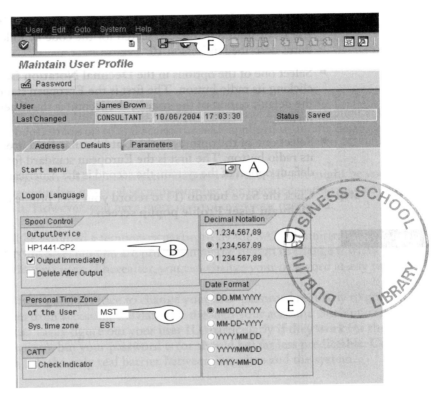

Figure 3.3 Enter default data for working with the system on the **Defaults subscreen** of the **Maintain User Profile screen**.

We recommend these actions:

- The **Start menu field** (A) enables you to set up the system to display a specific screen when you log on. Most users prefer to start with the **SAP Easy Access screen**. If this is your preference, leave this field blank.

    Some users routinely go to the same initial screen as soon as they log on to SAP. If this is the case with you, you can enter the transaction code[1] for that screen here so that it appears automatically when you log on.

---

1. See Part II for more instructions about transaction codes.

Lesson 5
NAVIGATING TO INITIAL SCREENS WITH THE MENU FOLDERS

This lesson describes the method of navigating to the initial screens of transactions with the **menu folders** of the **SAP Easy Access screen**.

The default version of the **SAP Easy Access screen** displays two sets of folders in its central work area: the **menu folders** and **Favorites folders** (Figure 5.1). These folders contain **links** (A) that lead you to the initial screens of transactions with just a double-click of the mouse.

The **menu folders** are exactly the same in their design and operation as the storage folders in your personal computer. They are organized in a *hierarchical* or *multilevel structure* of folders and subfolders. The lower-level or *lower-order* folders are generally few in number and define the general organization of the transaction links, separating them into broad *functional groups* such as *Human Resources* and *Accounting*. The higher-order folders, which are stored inside the lower-order ones, are far more numerous because they each represent a more narrowly defined functional group. At their highest level, they contain a small number of transaction links of a related type.

For example, consider the structure of the upper menu folder in the central work area of the **SAP Easy Access screen** in Figure 5.1.

- The first-order or *root folder* is called **SAP menu**. It contains a series of second-order folders for seven major functional groups: **Office**, **Cross-Application Components**, **Logistics**, **Accounting**, **Human Resources**, **Information Systems**, and **Tools**. The names and icons of these folders are indented to reflect their position in the folder hierarchy.

- The **Human Resources folder** opens to display four third-order folders: **Time Management**, **Payroll**, **Organizational Management**, and **Personnel Management** (Figure 5.2).

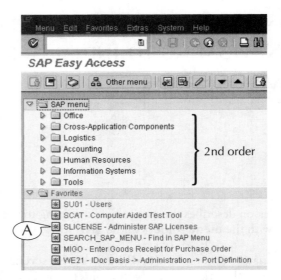

Figure 5.1 The first- and second-order folders of the **SAP Easy Access screen**. The transaction links of the **Favorites folders** are also displayed here (A). Notice that the folders and links are identified by different icons.

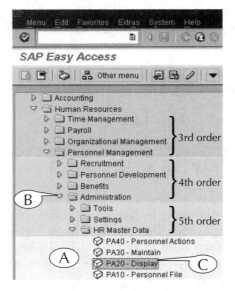

Figure 5.2 The higher-order folders and links in the **Human Resources folder** of our **SAP Easy Access screen**. Notice again the different icons of the folders and links.

- The **Personnel Management folder** opens to display four fourth-order folders: **Recruitment, Personnel Development, Benefits**, and **Administration**.

- The **Administration folder** opens to display three fifth-order folders for working with administrative data: **Tools, Settings**, and **HR Master Data**.

- The **HR Master Data folder** opens to display the links (A) to four transactions for reporting human resource data. Note the different icon for such links.

Navigating With the Menu Folds

ders, start at the olders and sub-initial screen.

pen (down)

er Data (PA20) esources, a Folder, then

he transaction.

Global Access Password List for students					
Resource	Web Address	Username	Password	IP Access	
Academic Search Premier - EBSCO	http://search.ebscohost.com	dublin	business	✔	
Business Source Premier - EBSCO	http://search.ebscohost.com	dublin	business	✔	
PEPArchive - EBSCO	http://search.ebscohost.com	dublin	business	✔	
PsycArticles - EBSCO	http://search.ebscohost.com	dublin	business	✔	
PsycInfo - EBSCO	http://search.ebscohost.com	dublin	business	✔	
Emerald	http://www.emeraldinsight.com	DBS	548169	✔	
LexisNexis	http://www.lexisnexis.com/uk/legal http://www.lexisnexis.com/uk/nexis	DBSLEXISNEXIS	CARMEL123	✔	
WARC	http://www.warc.com	WARC1103	DuBuSc	✔	

For example, the menu path for the *PA20 - Display transaction* would read:

SAP > Human Resources > Personnel Management > Administration > HR Master Data > PA20 - Display

SAP and User Menu Folders

Many SAP administrators provide two alternative sets of menu folders to their users: the **SAP menu folders** (Figure 5.1 and Figure 5.2) and the **User menu folders** (Figure 5.3).

The **SAP menu folders** contain links to the initial screens of every transaction[1] in all the installed modules in your system. They are basically the generic menu folders that come with the software.

For example, the **Human Resources folder** of the SAP menu holds the links for every transaction in a package of several modules that are used by organizations to manage their recruitment efforts, personnel, benefits, budgets and pensions, records, and time-entry data. Similarly, the **Accounting folder** holds the links for all the transactions in the Financial and Controlling modules, which are used to manage budgets and costs, and the **Logistics folder** holds the links for all the transactions in the Purchasing and Inventory modules (among others), which are used to manage the purchasing, storage, and inventory of equipment and consumable materials.

The **User menu folders** are custom-made by the SAP administrator for each user of their system. They store links to the initial screens of only those transactions that are used to do the company's business *and* which a given user is authorized to execute. The root folder of this folder set, **User menu** (Figure 5.3A), usually displays the name of that user.

For example, all employees in a company might be authorized to search the SAP database for a record of their work hours with the *Display HR Master Data (PA20)* transaction. If this is the case, their personal user menu folders will contain a subfolder, perhaps called *HR Master Data*, which holds a link to that transaction (Figure 5.3B).

You can choose to display either of the two sets of menu folders, along with the **Favorites folders**, with the first two buttons in the application toolbar of the **SAP Easy Access screen**.

- Click the first, the **User menu button** (C), to display your customized **User menu folders**.

- Click the second, the **SAP menu button** (D), to display the generic **SAP menu folders**.

---

1. The one exception is customized screens.

You can also follow the menu path **Menu > User menu** or **Menu > SAP menu** to display one of these two sets of menu folders.

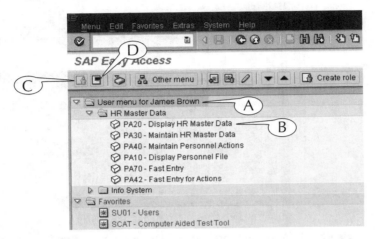

Figure 5.3   The **User menu** contains links to only those transactions that a particular user is allowed to execute.

Searching for Transactions

You can search the menu folders by keywords for specific folders and transaction links by using the **Find** (Figure 5.4A) and **Find again buttons** (B) of the standard toolbar. Follow this procedure.

Procedure

Searching for a Transaction With Keywords

Step 1. Click the **Find button** (A), *or*

Hit the **Ctrl + F keys** on your keyboard.

Step 2. The **Search in menu tree popup screen** appears (inset).

- Enter one or more keywords in the **Find field** (C). For this example, we entered *purchase order.*

- Select the *In texts option* (it should be preselected) so that the system searches the names of the transactions (D).

- Hit the **Enter key** on your keyboard.

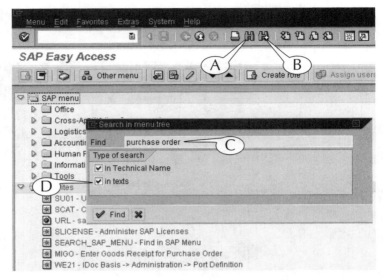

Figure 5.4   You can search for folders and transaction links with keywords via the **Search in menu tree screen**.

Step 3.   The system expands the menu folders and displays the first occurrence of the keywords (Figure 5.5A), which is highlighted.

- Click the **Find again button** (Figure 5.4B) *or* hit the **Ctrl + G keys** on your keyboard to locate the next occurrence of the keywords (Figure 5.5B).

- Continue until you find the folder or transaction link you are looking for.

You may wonder: *Why are there multiple occurrences of keywords?*

This reflects the integrated nature of the SAP modules. They are discrete building blocks of the system, like the bricks of a wall, but once they are hooked together, the boundaries between them disappear and you can communicate and move between them with great ease.

For instance, the transaction for creating purchase orders is a part of the Purchasing module, and thus you will find a link to its initial screen in that module's menu folders. However, warehouse operators, physical plant managers, administrative assistants, computer trainers, and many other business people need to order supplies, so there are also links to this same transaction in the **Warehouse**, **Plant Maintenance**, **Human Resources**, and **Learning Management folders**, among others.

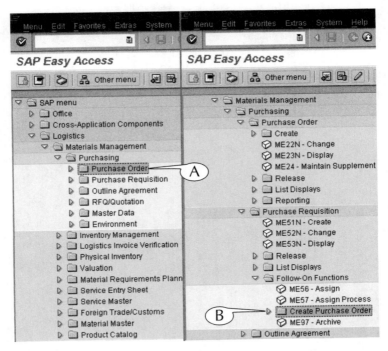

Figure 5.5   The search starts at the top of the menu folder and progresses steadily downward each time you click the **Find again button**. The results of the first two searches with the keywords "purchase order" are shown in these two screen images.

End Procedure

Lesson 6
NAVIGATING TO INITIAL SCREENS WITH THE FAVORITES FOLDERS

This lesson describes the creation, management, and use of the **Favorites folders** for navigating to the initial screens of transactions.

The default version of the **SAP Easy Access screen** displays two sets of **navigation folders** in its central work area: the **SAP** or **User menu folders** (see Lesson 5) and the **Favorites folders** (Figure 6.1). Both folder sets contain **links** to the initial screens of transactions and are organized in a multilevel or *hierarchical* structure of folders and subfolders. You can expand the folders to display their contents by either clicking their control arrows or double-clicking their names.

You have no control over the structure and contents of the **SAP** and **User menu folders** on your **SAP Easy Access screen**. The **SAP menu folders** are generic components of the software: They contain links to the initial screens of *every* transaction in the modules in your system. And the **User menu folders** are created by your SAP administrator to hold links to the initial screens of *only* those transactions that you are authorized to execute, and no others.

However, you have *total* control over your **Favorites folders**. You can create their structure of folders and subfolders, and you can control their contents, which can include links to any of your favorite or frequently run transactions as well as links to your favorite Web pages and e-mail system.

Figure 6.1 is an example of the **Favorites folders** that was created by a physical plant manager in a shipping company. Notice its structure and contents:

- There are four folders for the manager's favorite work management, material management, finance (budget and cost), and purchasing transaction links (A). Because he uses a small number of transactions in his work, most of these links are displayed with one double-click of a folder's name. This is a good design philosophy for your favorites: The links should be only one or two clicks of a folder away.

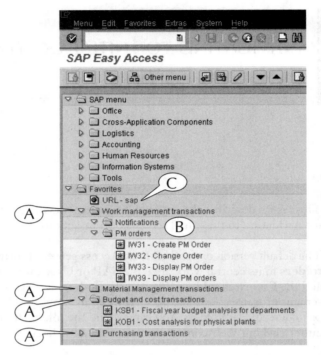

Figure 6.1 Favorite transactions are close at hand when their links are put in the **Favorites folders**.

- He created two subfolders, **Notifications** and **PM orders**, to hold links for two distinct groups of work management transactions (B).

- He created a link to a Web site (C), where he can search for and download SAP job aids, cheat sheets, and other support materials.

The **Favorites folders** provide quick "point and click" or *mouse-directed* navigation from the **SAP Easy Access screen** to the initial screens of transactions (and other places). This lesson describes the tools and procedures for creating and managing them and their contents.

Working With the Favorites Folders

Following are the five tools for creating and managing your **Favorites folders** and their links:

- **Favorites menu**
- Favorites shortcut menus
- Command buttons of the application toolbar
- Keystrokes
- Mouse

Favorites Menu

The **Favorites menu** of the main menu bar contains all the available commands for creating and managing the **Favorites folders** and their links (Figure 6.2).

- *Add*: adds transaction links to folders.
- *Change:* renames folders and links.
- *Move up* and *Move down*: rearrange the order of folders and links.
- *Delete*: deletes folders and links.
- *Insert folder*: creates new folders.
- *Insert transaction*: adds transaction links to folders by using their transaction codes.
- *Add other objects*: adds links to Web links, mail systems and other destinations to folders.
- *Download to PC*: downloads the **Favorites folders** to your personal computer or another external storage site.
- *Upload from PC*: uploads the **Favorites folders** from your personal computer or another external storage site.

To use the **Favorites menu** to manage your folders and links, you will usually follow this simple procedure:

- Click the *object* of the command (a folder or a link) to select and highlight it (A).
- Follow the menu path **Favorites > [Command]** to execute it on that object.

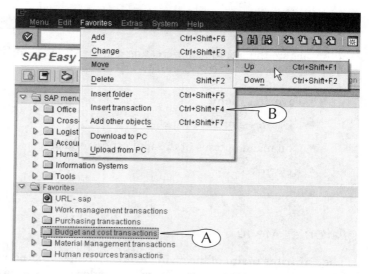

Figure 6.2   Select and highlight the object of the command, then select the command from the **Favorites menu** to execute it.

Shortcut Menus

Three shortcut menus together contain all the available commands for creating and managing the **Favorites folders** and their links. You can display them by right-clicking the folders and links (Figure 6.3).

- Right-click the **Favorites root folder** for a menu of commands for adding and deleting folders, links, and other objects to this folder (A).

- Right-click the higher-order folders for a menu of commands for managing them and their contents (B).

- Right-click the links for a menu of commands for working with them, along with commands for navigating to initial screens and adding shortcuts to your desktop (C).

To use the shortcut menus to manage your folders and links:

- *Right-click* the object of the command to select and highlight it (D) and simultaneously display its menu (C).

- Scroll down this menu and *left-click* a command to execute it on the object.

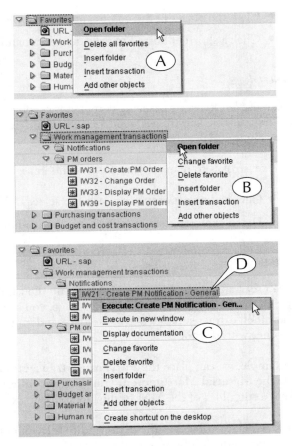

Figure 6.3 The three shortcut menus for working with the **Favorites folders**.

Application Toolbar

The last five buttons in the application toolbar of the **SAP Easy Access screen** (Figure 6.4) provide shortcuts for the *Add*, *Delete*, *Change*, *Move down*, and *Move up commands* of the **Favorites menu**. You can use them to manage your folders and links as you would that menu.

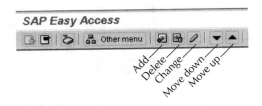

Figure 6.4 The five favorites shortcut buttons of the application toolbar.

- Click the object of the command to select and highlight it.
- Click a shortcut button to execute a command on that object.

Keystrokes

You can use keystrokes to execute commands on objects in your **Favorites folders**. The available keystrokes are identified on the right side of the **Favorites menu** (Figure 6.2B).

To use keystrokes to manage your folders and links:

- Click the object of the command to select and highlight it (Figure 6.2A).
- Hit the keystrokes to execute the command on that object.

Mouse

You can rearrange your **Favorites folders** and their links by clicking-and-dragging them with your mouse. For instance, you can insert folders inside one another, extract subfolders from folders, and move links from one folder to another with this tool.

For example, we can place the **Purchasing transactions folder** in Figure 6.5 inside the **Material Management transactions folder** (in other words, we can make it a subfolder of the **MM folder**) by following these steps:

Step 1. Click the object of the command to select and highlight it (A), and hold down the left button on the mouse.

Step 2. Drag the cursor towards the new "home" for the object. While it is moving toward its destination, a small box appears on the end of the cursor (B).

Step 3. When the cursor lands on its destination, the folder is outlined with a dashed box (C). Release the object there by releasing the mouse button.

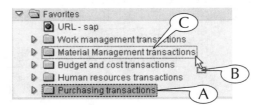

Figure 6.5 Clicking-and-dragging one **Favorites folder** into another.

We could reverse this process and put the **Purchasing transactions folder** on the same level as the **MM folder** by clicking-and-dragging the **Purchasing transactions folder** into the **Favorites root folder**.

SAP accommodates the varied preferences of its users by providing several keyboard- and mouse-directed methods for working in its application window. This is especially true with the **Favorites folders**: It provides three complete menus—the mouse-driven Favorites and shortcut menus, along with keystrokes—for creating and managing favorites, along with five shortcut buttons and a mousing technique.

With so many choices, which do you choose?

If you prefer to work with the mouse, the shortcut menus are the most efficient tools for working with your favorites.

- They contain *every* available command for working with the folders and links;
- They are displayed *automatically* when you select and highlight the object of a command; *and*
- They appear *right next to* the object of a command, so they are easy to reach and select.

The **Favorites menu** also contains every command for working with the folders and links, but it does require more "mousing" across the **SAP Easy Access screen** to use: You must first select the object of a command in the central work area, then move up to the menu bar and scroll down the **Favorites menu** to execute that command. The usefulness of this menu is further diminished by the application toolbar, which contains handy shortcut buttons for five of the ten commands in the **Favorites menu**.

We do not want to impose our preferences on the readers. Consequently, we provide instructions for several possible methods of working with the **Favorites folders** in the following sets of procedures, and let you decide which of them to use.

Adding Favorites Folders

The first step in working with the **Favorites folders** is to design and create its structure by adding folders and subfolders to the **Favorites root folder**. The basic design philosophy is to create the *least* number of levels in a structure so that your favorite links are just one or two clicks away—in other words, to keep the menu paths short.

Figure 6.6 shows a set of **Favorites folders** with a second level of folders for four distinct classes of transactions. We can insert a new subfolder called **Time entry transactions** inside the **Human resources folder** by following this procedure.

Procedure

Creating a Favorites Folder

Step 1. Click the intended destination of the new folder to select and highlight it (Figure 6.6A), then follow the menu path **Favorites > Insert folder**, *or*

Right-click the destination of the new folder, then select the *Insert folder command* from the shortcut menu.

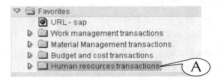

Figure 6.6   Select the location for a new favorites folder.

Step 2. The **Creating a Folder in the Favorite List popup screen** appears (Figure 6.7).

- Enter a name for the new folder in the **Folder name field** (A).

- Hit the **Enter key** on your keyboard.

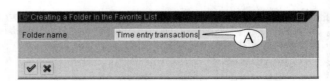

Figure 6.7   Enter a name for the new folder on this screen.

Step 3. The new folder appears in its selected spot (Figure 6.8A).

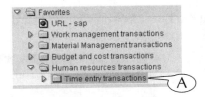

Figure 6.8   The new folder appears inside the selected folder.

End Procedure

Adding Transaction Links to the Favorites Folders

Once you create your folders and subfolders, you can add transaction links to them in one of two ways, depending on whether or not you know their transaction codes (see the next lesson for an explanation of transaction codes and how to display them on the **SAP Easy Access screen**).

For an example, we insert a link for the *List-Display Purchase Requisitions transaction*, which has the transaction code *ME5A*, into the **Purchasing transactions folder** in both of these ways.

Procedure

Adding a Transaction Link With Its Code to the Favorites Folder

Step 1.   Click the intended destination of the link to select and highlight it (Figure 6.9A), then follow the menu path **Favorites > Insert transaction**, *or*

Right-click the destination of the link, then select the *Insert transaction command* from the shortcut menu.

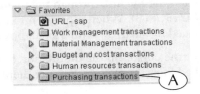

Figure 6.9   Select the location for the new favorites link.

Step 2. The **Manual entry of a transaction popup screen** appears (Figure 6.10).

- Enter the transaction code in the **Transaction code field** (A).
- Hit the **Enter key** on your keyboard.

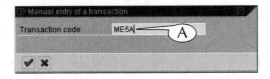

Figure 6.10   Enter the transaction code on this screen.

Step 3. The new link appears in its selected spot (Figure 6.11A).

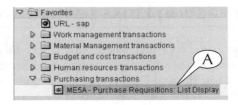

Figure 6.11   The new link appears inside the selected folder.

End Procedure

Procedure

Adding a Transaction Link Without Its Code to the Favorites Folder

Step 1. Follow the menu path through the **SAP menu folders** or **User menu folders** to the link for the transaction (Figure 6.12A).

Step 2. Click-and-drag the link toward its destination in the **Favorites folders**.

As you slide the link through the menu folders, the cursor appears as a *slashed circle* (B). When it passes into the **Favorites folders**, the circle is replaced by an arrow with a small box attached to its end (C).

Step 3. Point the cursor on the destination folder, and its name is outlined by a dashed line (D). Release the link there by releasing your mouse button.

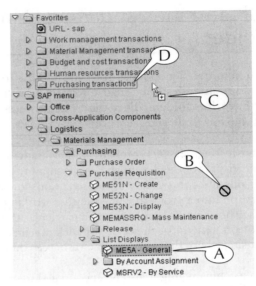

Figure 6.12   Click-and-drag a copy of a transaction link from the menu folders to your **Favorites folders**.

Step 4.   A copy of the transaction link appears in the **Favorites folders** (Figure 6.13A); the original link still appears in the menu folders (B).

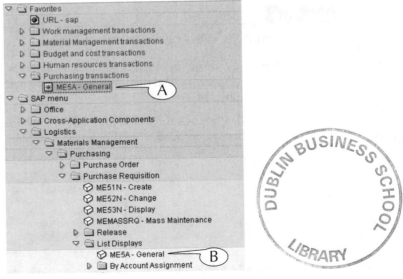

Figure 6.13   The transaction link is copied, not moved, into the selected folder.

End Procedure

Adding Web, Intranet, and E-mail Links to the Favorites Folders

In addition to transaction links, you can add links to other objects, including Web and Intranet sites and e-mail applications such as *MS Outlook* and *Eudora*, to your **Favorites folders**. They can be handy tools for collecting and distributing information while you are working with SAP.

For instance, the users in a company might be advised to create a favorites link to the Intranet sites of their company's SAP support groups, where they can download job aids and cheat sheets with instructions for working with the system. If the users run into a problem while they are working with the system—for example, if they don't know how to set up a particular transaction or how to print the output of a transaction—they can just click this link to jump immediately to that Intranet site, where they will find the resources they need.

Users in a company might also be encouraged to create favorite links to useful Web sites such as *America's SAP Users Group* (*www.asug.com*), an organization that provides resources, advice, and information to SAP users around the country, and SAP's corporate Web site (*www.sap.com*), where users can find information about their products and links to other support and resource sites. We create a link to this second Web site in the following procedure.

Procedure

Adding a Web or an Intranet Link to the Favorites Folders

Step 1. Click the intended destination of the new link to select and highlight it (Figure 6.14A), then follow the menu path **Favorites > Add other objects**, *or*

Right-click the destination of the new link, then select the *Add other objects command* from the shortcut menu.

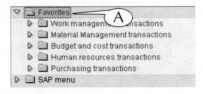

Figure 6.14   Select the location for the new Web/Intranet link.

Step 2. The **Add additional objects popup screen** appears (Figure 6.15).

- Select the *Web address or file option* (A) if it is not already selected by default.

- Hit the **Enter key** on your keyboard.

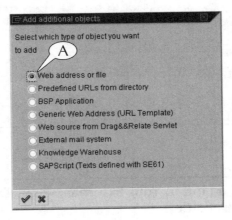

Figure 6.15   Select the type of link.

Step 3. The **Add a Web address or file path popup screen** appears (Figure 6.16).

- Enter a name for the link in the **Text field** (A).

- Enter the URL—the Web or Intranet address—in the **Web address or file field** (B). For this example, we entered *www.sap.com*.

  Note: You can also highlight the address in the address field of your Web browser, copy it with the keystroke **Ctrl + C**, then paste it in the field with the keystroke **Ctrl + V**.

- Hit the **Enter key** on your keyboard.

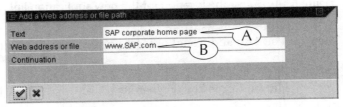

Figure 6.16   Enter a name and address for the new favorite link on this screen.

Step 4. The Web link (A) appears in the selected spot in your **Favorites folders** (Figure 6.17).

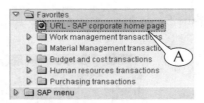

Figure 6.17   The new Web link appears in the selected folder.

End Procedure

Procedure

Adding a Link to Your External E-mail Application in the Favorites Folders

Step 1. Click the intended destination of the new link to select and highlight it (Figure 6.18A), then follow the menu path **Favorites > Add other objects**, *or*

Right-click the destination of the new link, then select the *Add other objects* command from the shortcut menu.

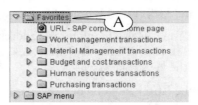

Figure 6.18   Select the location for the new application link.

Step 2. The **Add additional objects popup screen** appears (Figure 6.19).

- Select the *External mail system option* (A).

- Hit the **Enter key** on your keyboard.

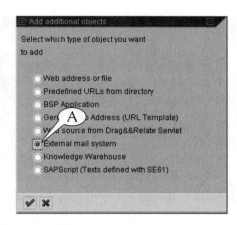

Figure 6.19 Select the type of link.

Step 3. The **Change node popup screen** appears (Figure 6.20).

■ Enter a name for the link in the **Text field** (A).

■ Click inside the **Object description field** to call up its search button (B), then click that button.

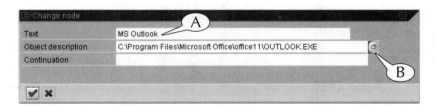

Figure 6.20 Enter a name for the new link.

Step 4. The **Open screen** of your computer's operating system appears (Figure 6.21).

■ Locate the *Execute file* of your e-mail application (it will probably be in the **Programs folder** of your computer). The file name usually consists of the application name (*Outlook* in this example) followed by *.exe*.

■ Click the *Execute file* to select and highlight it (A), then click the **Open button** (B).

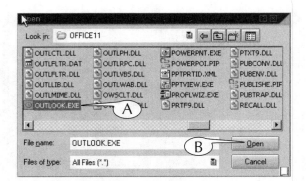

Figure 6.21   Select the execution file of the e-mail application.

Step 5.   The path to the *Execute file* is entered in the **Object description field** of the **Change node screen** (Figure 6.20).

- Hit the **Enter key** on your keyboard, and the link appears in the selected spot in the **Favorites folders** (Figure 6.22A).

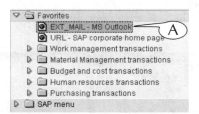

Figure 6.22   The new application link appears in the selected folder.

End Procedure

Changing the Names of Favorites Folders and Links

You can change the names of folders and links in your **Favorites folders** at any time. For example, you may want to rearrange your folders and then rename them to reflect their new order, or you may want to rename a transaction link to something that is more distinctive or accurate.

It is, in fact, fairly common to change the names of favorite transaction links as soon as you create them. When you add links to the **Favorites folders**, they are given default names by the system, and sometimes these names are vague or too wordy.

For instance, there is a transaction in the Plant Maintenance module that creates a work order, technically called a *Plant Maintenance* or *PM order*, for installing and repairing equipment. When you create a favorite link for this transaction, it bears the name *Create Order* by default.

But this name is vague, because there are several other types of orders in other modules of SAP, including purchase orders, internal orders, and sales orders. More precision in its name would help distinguish this PM order transaction link from those of other types of orders.

Another example: there is a transaction in the Controlling module that displays planned expenses and actual costs—that is, a budget—for a group or department in a business enterprise. A favorite link for this transaction bears the default name *Cost Center Actual/Plan/Variance*, but *Budget Report* would be a better name, and a shorter one too.

Follow this next procedure for changing the names of **Favorites folders** and links.

Changing the Name of a Folder or Link in the Favorites Folders

Step 1. Click the object of the command to select and highlight it (A), then click the **Change button** in the application toolbar (Figure 6.23), *or*

Click the object of the command, then follow the menu path **Favorites > Change**, *or*

Right-click the object of the command, then select the *Change command* from the shortcut menu.

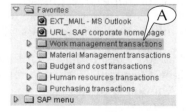

Figure 6.23   Select the location for the new link.

Step 2. The **Change a favorite popup screen** appears (Figure 6.24).

- Enter a new name for the object in the **Text field** (A).
- Hit the **Enter key** on your keyboard.

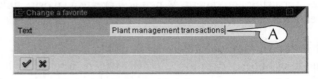

Figure 6.24   Enter the new name of the object.

Step 3. The object's new name appears in your **Favorites folders** (Figure 6.25A).

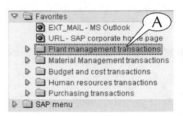

Figure 6.25   The object is renamed.

End Procedure

You can shuffle and organize the contents of your **Favorites folders** at any time with your mouse and the buttons of the application toolbar.

You can arrange your **Favorites folders** and their links easily by clicking-and-dragging them into new positions. For instance, you can click-and-drag folders into other folders, pull subfolders out of other folders, and move links in and out of folders, all with this tool.

You can change the list order of a folder or link by clicking it to select and highlight it (Figure 6.26A) and then clicking the **Move down** (B) or **Move up** (C) **button** in the application toolbar to move it down or up the folder list (D).

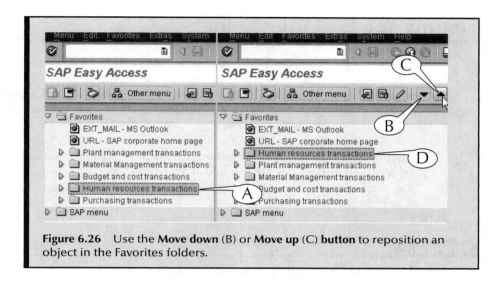

Figure 6.26   Use the **Move down** (B) or **Move up** (C) **button** to reposition an object in the Favorites folders.

Deleting Favorites Folders and Links

You can delete your **Favorites folders** (all but the root folder) and links in three ways:

- Click the object of the command to select and highlight it (A), then click the **Delete button** (B) in the application toolbar (Figure 6.27), *or*

- Click the name of the object, then follow the menu command **Favorites > Delete** (C), *or*

- Right-click the name of the object, then select the *Delete command* from the shortcut menu.

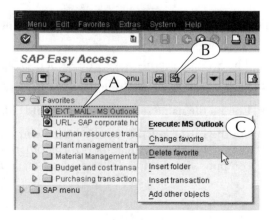

Figure 6.27   Deleting an object in the **Favorites folders**.

Sharing Your Favorites Folders

You can easily share your **Favorites folders** with other users. You can download its contents into your personal computer and store it in a file there. You can then e-mail it to your colleagues, who can upload it from their personal computer into the **Favorites folders** of their **SAP Easy Access screen** and then work with the same transactions that you use.

Follow these next two procedures for downloading and uploading favorites. For both procedures, we use the example of a favorites file that is downloaded into, and then uploaded from, the storage folders of a personal computer running the *Windows* operating system.

Downloading Your Favorites Folders

Step 1. Follow the menu path **Favorites > Download to PC** to download your **Favorites folders** (Figure 6.28).

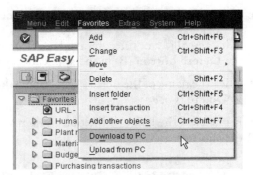

Figure 6.28   Menu path for downloading your **Favorites folders**.

Step 2. The **SAP Custom – Save File As screen** appears (Figure 6.29).

- Select a storage location in the **Save in field** (A).

- Enter a file name in the **File name field** (B).

- Hit the **Enter key** on your keyboard, and the file appears in the selected storage location in a plain text format that can be read by any personal computer. Send it to a colleague by e-mail or other means (e.g., disk).

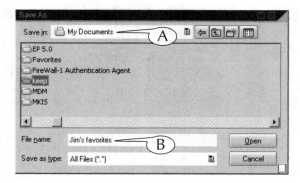

Figure 6.29   Save your **Favorites folders** as a file on your personal computer.

End Procedure

Procedure

Uploading Favorites Folders

Step 1. Follow the menu path **Favorites > Upload from PC** to upload a favorites file from your personal computer (Figure 6.30).

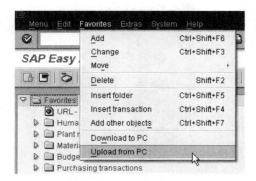

Figure 6.30   Menu path for uploading a favorites file into your **Favorites folders**.

Step 2. The **Open screen** appears (Figure 6.31).

- Locate the favorites file in your personal computer's storage folders (A) and double-click it to upload it into your **Favorites folders**.

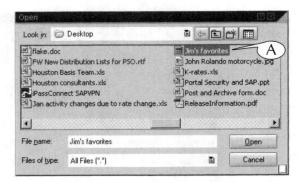

Figure 6.31   Select the file with the **Favorites folders** on your personal computer.

End Procedure

Lesson 7

NAVIGATING TO INITIAL SCREENS WITH TRANSACTION CODES

This lesson describes the use of **transaction codes** to navigate to the initial screens of transactions.

Every SAP transaction is assigned its own unique transaction code or *t-code*, which is often used as a shorthand name for the transaction itself. The codes are usually four or five characters long, although they can be longer, and they are organized according to their functions, which are often indicated in the transaction code itself. For example:

- Purchasing transactions have four- and five-character codes that begin with *ME*. For instance, you can create a purchase requisition with the *ME51N transaction*, display a list of requisitions from your department with the *ME5A transaction*, and create a vendor purchase order for an approved requisition with the *ME59 transaction*.

- Equipment-maintenance transactions have four-character codes that begin with *IW*. For instance, you can create a work order for maintaining a vehicle with the *IW31 transaction*, display the costs of that work with the *IW33 transaction*, and close the books on the work with the *IW32* transaction.

- Reporting transactions often have very long codes because there are so many varieties of them. For instance, you can display a yearly budget for a department with the *S_ALR_87013611 transaction* and a yearly budget for a large work project with the *S_ALR_87013543 transaction*. But you can also display the *monthly* budget of a project with the *S_ALR_87013614 transaction* and display the budget for each *contractor* working on that project with the *S_ALR_87013615 transaction*.

You can navigate to the initial screen of transactions by entering their transaction code in the **command fields** of screens. This navigation method can be used on the **SAP Easy Access screen**, where it provides a rapid, keyboard-driven alternative to pointing-and-clicking through the menu or favorites folders to a transaction link, as well as on any initial or output screen.

Navigating With Transaction Codes

To navigate from the **SAP Easy Access screen** to the initial screen of any transaction, simply enter its transaction code in the **command field** (Figure 7.1A), then hit the **Enter key** on your keyboard, and the initial screen appears.

Figure 7.1   Entering a transaction code in the **command field** of the **SAP Easy Access** screen.

To navigate from any other screen (initial or output) to the initial screen of any transaction, enter the prefix */n* or */o*, followed by the transaction code, in the **command field** and hit the **Enter key** on your keyboard (Figure 7.2). The prefix instructs the system that you are interrupting the present transaction to start a new one.

- When you attach the */n* prefix to a transaction code (A), the initial screen of the new transaction is displayed inside the existing application window.

- When you attach the */o* prefix to a transaction code (B), the initial screen of the new transaction is displayed inside a new application window, which is automatically opened by the system.

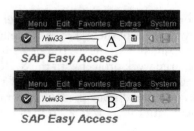

Figure 7.2   Navigating from other screens to start a new transaction in the same application window (A) or in a new application window (B).

You can also select and enter a transaction code in the **command field** from its **list menu**, where your most recently entered transaction codes are recorded. Just follow this next procedure.

Selecting Transaction Codes From the Command Field List Menu

Step 1. Click the list icon at the right end of the **command field** (Figure 7.3A) to display a list menu of recently entered transaction codes (B).

Step 2. Scroll down the menu and click a transaction code, and it is entered in the command field.

Note: You must follow the usual protocol when you are making this selection: select a raw transaction code (for example, *IW33*) whenever you are navigating from the **SAP Easy Access screen**, or an appended code (for example: */nIW33* or */oIW33*) whenever you are navigating from any other screen.

Step 3. Hit the **Enter key** on your keyboard, and the initial screen appears.

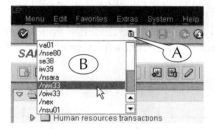

Figure 7.3   Selecting a transaction code from the list menu of the **command field**.

Finally, you can manage the application window by entering the following codes in the **command field**:

- Enter */n* and hit the **Enter key** to end a transaction. The system returns you to the **SAP Easy Access screen** *without* asking you to confirm this action, and any data that you entered on the transaction screens is *not* saved.

- Enter */i* and hit the **Enter key** to close a single application window. If there is only one open window, you are asked to confirm that you want to close it and thereby log off from the system.

- Enter */nex* and hit the **Enter key** to close all your open application windows and log off the system. The system does *not* ask you to confirm this action before you are logged off.

- Enter */nend* and hit the **Enter key** to close all your open application windows and log off the system. The system *does* ask you to confirm this action before you are logged off.

Identifying Transaction Codes

Generally, many users learn the transaction codes for the transactions they use for their work from other users in their department or group, as well as from job aids, cheat sheets, and other tools that document the procedures for executing transactions. This mode of communication is made easier by the common use of transaction codes as shorthand names for transactions. For instance, a new employee in a department may be instructed by their manager to enter employees' work-time data in SAP by "running the *CATS2 transaction*" or asked to generate a list of pending work orders by "running the *IW39 transaction*."

However, you can also identify transaction codes on-screen in several ways.

First, you can display the transaction codes of transactions alongside their names in the **menu** and **Favorites folders** of the **SAP Easy Access screen** by following this procedure.

Procedure

Displaying Transaction Codes on the SAP Easy Access Screen

Step 1. Follow the menu path **Extras > Settings** (Figure 7.4A).

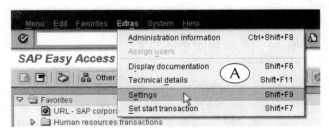

Figure 7.4   Menu path for calling up the **Settings popup screen**.

Step 2. The **Settings popup screen** appears (Figure 7.5).

- Select the *Display technical names option* (A).

- Hit the **Enter key** on your keyboard.

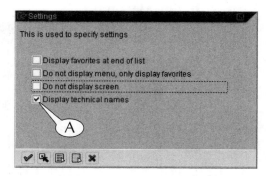

Figure 7.5   Settings popup screen.

Step 3. The transaction codes (A) appear ahead of the transaction links in the **menu** and **Favorites folders** (Figure 7.6).

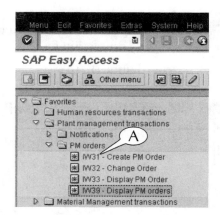

Figure 7.6   The transaction links of the navigation folders now show their transaction codes.

End Procedure

You can also display the code of a transaction from any screen (initial or output) of that transaction through the menu bar or the system data field of the status bar by following these next procedures.

Identifying Transaction Codes With the Menu Bar

Step 1. Follow the menu path **System > Status** (Figure 7.7A).

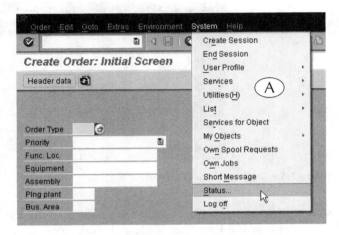

Figure 7.7   Calling up the **Status popup screen** through the System menu.

Step 2. The **Status popup screen** appears (Figure 7.8). The transaction code is displayed in the **Transaction field** (A).

Step 3. Click the close button (B) to erase the **Status popup screen**.

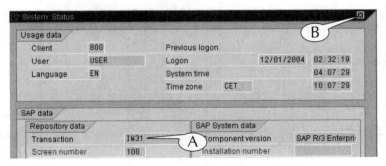

Figure 7.8   The **System status popup screen** displays a wealth of mostly technical information—and the transaction code of the main screen.

Procedure

Identifying Transaction Codes With the Status Bar

Step 1. Click the list icon (Figure 7.9A) in the system data field, which lies at the right end of the status bar.

Step 2. The **system data menu** appears with the transaction code (B).

> *Note:* If you scroll down and select *Transaction* on this menu so that a check mark appears to its left, the transaction code of the screens will always appear in the status bar of all your screens.

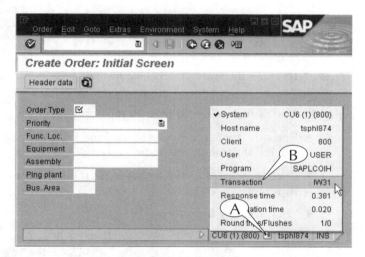

Figure 7.9   The **system data menu** displays the transaction code of a screen.

End Procedure

Searching for Transactions by Transaction Codes

You can search the menu folders and transaction links by transaction code with the **Find button** (A) of the standard toolbar (Figure 7.10). Follow this next procedure.

Procedure

Searching for Transactions With Keywords

Step 1. Click the **Find button** (A), *or*

- Hit the **Ctrl + F keys** on your keyboard.

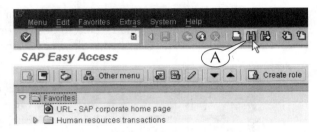

Figure 7.10   Start the search by clicking the Find button (A).

Step 2. The **Search in menu tree popup screen** appears (Figure 7.11).

- Enter the transaction code in the **Find field** (A). For this example, we entered the transaction code *ME51N*.

- Select the *In Technical Name option* (if it is not already selected) to search by transaction code (B).

- Hit the **Enter key** on your keyboard.

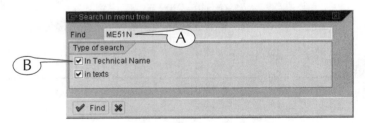

Figure 7.11   Search for transaction links by transaction codes with the **Search in menu tree popup screen**.

Step 3. The system expands the menu folders and displays the first occurrence of the transaction code (A), which is highlighted (Figure 7.12).

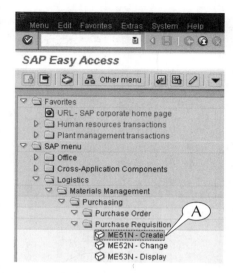

Figure 7.12   The system locates the first occurrence of the transaction code in the menu folder.

End Procedure

Transaction codes are generally the fastest, most convenient way to navigate to the initial screens of transactions. You can only navigate with the **menu folders** and **Favorites folders** from the **SAP Easy Access screen**, but you can navigate with transaction codes from *any* screen, including the initial and output screens of transactions. In addition, you do not have to navigate by pointing-and-clicking your way through a long, hard-to-remember menu path; rather, you simply enter a short code in the command field and hit the **Enter key** on your keyboard to reach your destination.

For this reason, we recommend that you learn to navigate with transaction codes. To remember them, write the names and codes of your favorite transactions on an index card and post it on or near your computer monitor for handy reference—not the most high-tech solution, we admit, but it works for us.

However, we mentioned at the beginning of this lesson that there are certain classes of reporting transactions that have very long transaction codes. These transactions are the exception to the rule about the supremacy of transaction codes, for even the most adept typist will often err in entering such long codes in the command field. We recommend that you create and use links in your **Favorites folders** to navigate to the initial screens of these transactions.

Lesson 8

NAVIGATING BETWEEN SCREENS WITH MENU BARS

The last three lessons discussed three methods for navigating to the initial screens of transactions from the **SAP Easy Access screen**. This last lesson concludes this discussion with a brief mention of navigating to initial screens of transactions from other initial and output screens.

Consider these two situations:

- Situation 1: You navigate from the **SAP Easy Access screen** to the initial screen of a transaction with transaction codes or links, only to realize that you went to the wrong screen. You wanted the initial screen of a transaction that *displays* the data on an object, but instead you mistakenly navigated to the initial screen of the transaction that *creates* the data record for that object.

- Situation 2: You execute a transaction that displays the data on an object. Once you see those data, you decide to execute another related transaction on that same object.

In both situations, you could either return to the **SAP Easy Access screen** and find the correct link for the next transaction in the menu folders, or you could enter the transaction code for its initial screen in the command field to move there. However, there is a third alternative: you can use the menu bar of the screen in front of you to navigate to the desired one.

This short lesson provides some examples of using the menu bar for this purpose.

Navigating from the Initial Screen of a Transaction

You can navigate from one initial screen to another initial screen for a related transaction via the **object menu**. This is the first menu in the menu bars of many initial screens, and it contains a set of commands for navigating to the initial screens of related transactions. They are not present on every initial screen, but where they are, object menus are handy navigation shortcuts.

For example, suppose you call up the initial screen of the *Display Equipment (IE03) transaction*, and then realize you meant to call up the initial screen of the *Change Equipment transaction*. You can use the object menu of the first screen to take a shortcut to the second one: click it to display its commands, then select the *Change command* (Figure 8.1A).

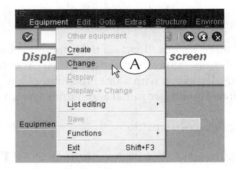

Figure 8.1   The object menu of the **Display equipment initial screen** (its name is partly hidden behind the menu) contains commands that lead you to the initial screens of other equipment transactions, including the **Change equipment initial screen**.

For another example, suppose you call up the initial screen of the *Display Material (MM03) transaction*, but then decide to navigate to the initial screen of the *Change Material transaction* instead. Once again, you can select the *Change command* from the object menu of the first screen to jump to the second (Figure 8.2A).

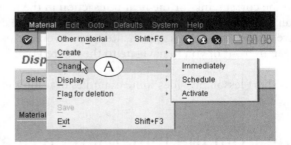

Figure 8.2   The object menu of the **Display Material initial screen** (its name is partly hidden behind the menu) contains commands that lead you to the initial screens of other material transactions. We are selecting the *Change command* in this example.

Navigating from the Output Screen of a Transaction

We use the example of an equipment display transaction to illustrate the method of navigating from the output screen of one transaction to the initial screen of a related transaction.

The output screen for the *Display equipment (IE03) transaction* (Figure 8.3) displays technical and logistical data on a piece of equipment (in this case, equipment number *10005662*), including its make, model, serial number, purchase price, and the plant that is responsible for its installation and operation. However, the output does not contain data on its maintenance history, such as the number of times it was sent to a maintenance shop and the repair work done during those visits. This sort of data appears in the *plant maintenance* (or *PM*) *order* records for the equipment.

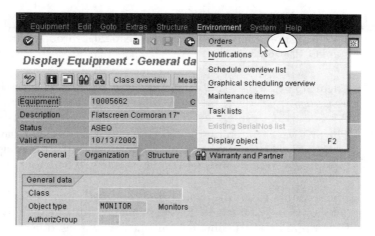

Figure 8.3   The **Display equipment output screen** and the **Environment menu**. This menu leads you to the initial screens of other transactions that you can execute to gather different types of data about the equipment.

You can display a list of all the plant-maintenance orders for this equipment with the *Display PM Order (IW39) transaction*. For this purpose, you call up the initial screen of that transaction (Figure 8.4), enter the equipment code in the **Equipment field** (A), and execute it.

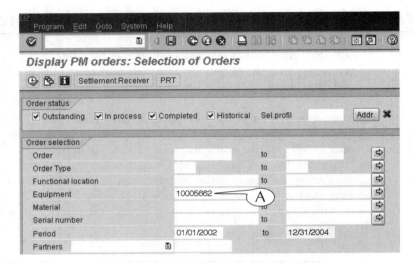

Figure 8.4   The initial screen for displaying a list of PM orders. This screen is set to display a list of orders for the calendar years 2002 through 2004 for equipment number 10005662.

There are two ways to call up the initial screen of the *Display PM Order (IW39) transaction*.

The first way is to return to the **SAP Easy Access screen**, navigate from there to the initial screen of the transaction, manually enter the equipment code in the **Equipment field** (Figure 8.4A), and execute it. That's four steps.

The second is to use the menu bar of the *Display equipment (IE03) transaction* output screen (Figure 8.3). This bar contains three menus—**Goto**, **Extras**, and **Environment**—that contain commands for starting other transactions which report data on the equipment in question. For this particular case, you would display the **Environment menu** (A), from which you would then select the *Orders command*.

This action takes you immediately to the initial screen of the *Display PM Order transaction* (Figure 8.4), where you will find that the equipment code is already entered in the **Equipment field** (A). Once there, all you need to do is execute the transaction. That's just two steps.

Exploring SAP

The **Environment menu** and other "shortcut menus" to related transactions can be found on many output screens, but unlike the object menu of initial screens, they are neither consistently named nor placed in the menu bar. You may receive instructions in the form of a job aid that alerts you to their availability and functions, but if not, you should simply explore the menu bars of output screens and test out the available commands you find there.

What, are you crazy, you might be thinking, *just start executing commands at random in SAP?* The answer is *Yes. SAP is not Dr. Strangelove, and you can learn a lot by experimenting.*

You will not crash computer servers, bankrupt your company, or launch a nuclear missile strike by exploring the functions of the commands in the menu bars of output screens or, for that matter, by experimenting with the many menu commands, buttons, popup screens, and other screen elements that you might encounter with this software and which we do not have time or space to describe in this book. The system has all sorts of safeguards to protect itself, its database, and the global village from you.

For example, if you are not authorized to execute a particular transaction, you will not be able to execute it from an initial or output screen, just as you will not be able to execute it from the **SAP Easy Access screen**.

Similarly, if a click of a button or a selection of a menu command triggers some sensitive process, such as placing a large purchase order with a vendor, granting a huge pay raise to your colleagues, or firing the CEO of your company, there are many built-in checks and approval processes in the SAP workflow to guarantee that the process is not carried out without approval from the appropriate authorities in your company.

To the contrary, you can learn a lot about SAP by exploring its functionality on your own. We are expert users of the system and have sat through many training classes and read many books about it. But we know that no book or class can tell you *everything* about this complex and sophisticated software—sometimes, you just have to play with it and see what else it can do. We have learned all sorts of tricks and capabilities in this manner, and we strongly encourage you to do the same.

Part III
SETTING UP INITIAL SCREENS

Before anything else, preparation is the key to success. — Alexander Graham Bell (American scientist)

Lesson 9
ENTERING CODES AND TEXT

White, read/write **data entry fields** are found on the initial screens of all SAP transactions, as well as search screens (described in the next lesson) and other procedural popup screens. They accept several types of data from you, including

- **Object codes**, which are alphanumerical codes for any objects, persons, and activities that are tracked by SAP, such as purchase requisitions, consumable materials, goods shipments, department budgets, and employees;
- **Date codes**, such as *01/01/2004* (January 1, 2004);
- **Unit-of-measure codes**, such as *USD* (US dollars) or *lbs* (pounds);
- **Text**, including short phrases such as *Equipment is damaged* or longer sentences and paragraphs.

Data entry fields appear in four formats on initial screens: **single fields**, **paired fields**, **line-item fields**, and **long-text fields**.

Single data fields allow you to enter either a single code for any object, date, or unit of measure or a short text phrase of any wording (Figure 9.1).

| Equipment | 10056442 | A |
| Short text | Transformer | B |

Figure 9.1   Single data fields for code (A) and text (B) entries.

Paired data fields, which are separated by the word *to*, give you the option of entering either one code or short-text entry in the first (left) field or a range of codes and text in both fields (Figure 9.2). When you enter a range of data in paired fields, they must be in ascending alphabetical or numerical order. For instance, when you enter object codes, you must enter the lower-numbered code in the first field and the higher-numbered one in the second (right) field.

For example, Figure 9.2 illustrates two different setups for the paired **Material fields**, in this case taken from the initial screen of a transaction that displays data about consumable materials. The first screen image (A) shows that only one code is entered in the first of the two fields. Consequently, this transaction will only display data about the one material with that object code. The second screen image (B) shows that a range of codes is entered in the paired fields. Consequently, this transaction will display data about every material with a code that falls inside this range.

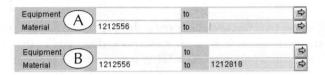

Figure 9.2   You can enter a single code (A) or a range of codes (B) in paired fields.

Line-item fields are strings of fields in which you can enter several bits of coded and short-text data about an object. For instance, the initial screen for a transaction that creates a requisition contains a table with several rows of line-item fields (Figure 9.3). Each row contains a string of fields in which you enter the details on one material or service that is being requisitioned, such as its description and code, the desired quantity and its unit of measure, and the delivery date.

Incidentally, notice that this line-item table is headed by an application toolbar (A). You can use this toolbar to sort, filter, and otherwise customize the data entries in the table. We describe the procedures for doing so in Part IV of this book.

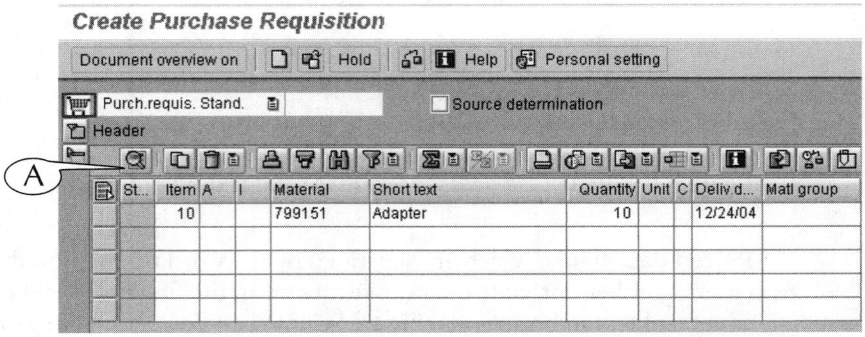

Figure 9.3   Line-item fields for entering coded and short-text data about a purchase requisition.

Long-text fields are read/write fields in which you enter many lines and paragraphs of text. In some cases, you can partition these text entries into different categories by using **text descriptors** that are attached to the field.

For instance, the initial screen for creating a requisition (Figure 9.4) contains a long-text field (A) for entering written information about a purchase. This field is accompanied by four text descriptors (B). Click the first one, *Item text*, and you can enter any general information about the requisition in the long-text field. Click another descriptor, such as *Delivery text*, and the item text disappears. You can now enter any information about the delivery in the long-text field.

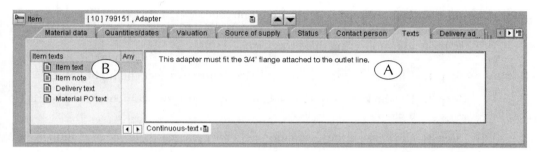

Figure 9.4   A long-text field (A) and its accompanying text descriptors (B). Click one of the text descriptors to enter or display different classes of text data.

Tips for Entering Codes and Text

Generally, you enter code or text in a data entry field by first clicking inside that field to select and highlight it and then typing your entry on your keyboard. However, there are some variations in this method that you should know.

Tip #1: Date and project codes contain several components that are separated by slashes (/). For example, date codes might be written in a *Month/Date/Year* format,[1] whereas project codes might be written in a format such as *Location/Year/Type/ID*.

When you are entering such codes into entry fields, however, you do not have to enter the slashes: simply enter the components of the codes (Figure 9.5A) and hit the **Enter key** on your keyboard, and the system automatically formats them correctly for you (Figure 9.5B).

---

1. Dates can also be entered in a *MM.DD.YY*, a *DD.MM.YY* or a *YY.MM.DD* format, among others. See Lesson 3 for instructions on setting your preferred formats for calendar dates.

Incidentally, whenever you hit the **Enter key** after *any* data entry, the system checks the database and verifies that the entry is a valid one. If it is not, the system alerts you to that effect with an error message.

Figure 9.5   Enter an abbreviated date (A) and hit the **Enter key**, and the system formats the date for you (B).

Tip #2: You can copy an entry from one source, such as other SAP screens and even the screens of other applications (such as *MS Word*), then paste it into an entry field by following this procedure.

Step 1.   Click-and-drag across the desired entry to select and highlight it.

Step 2.   Hit the keystroke **Ctrl + C** to copy it into your computer's clipboard memory.

Step 3.   Click inside the destination field for the entry to select and highlight it.

Step 4.   Hit the keystroke **Ctrl + V** to paste it into the field.

Tip #3: Some data entry fields only accept a limited number of predefined entries (called *possible entries* by SAP), which are set up by your SAP administrator. When this situation exists, the field bears a **list icon** at its right end (Figure 9.6A). You can enter one of the predefined entries (and no others) by following this two-step procedure.

Step 1.   Click the icon (A) to display a menu of the available entries (B).

Step 2.   Scroll down the list to the desired entry and click it, and it is entered automatically in the field.

Figure 9.6   The **Title field** accepts only four entries. Click the **list icon** (A) to select one of them from a list (B).

Tip #4: You can move quickly from one data entry field to the next on any screen with the **Tab key** on your keyboard instead of using your mouse. When the cursor is sitting inside one field, hit the **Tab key** to move to the next available field on the screen, or use the **Shift + Tab key** to move to the previous field.

Tip #5: When you click (or tab) inside a data entry field, it is highlighted, and a small **search button** (A) appears to its right (Figure 9.7A). You can click this button to call up a search screen, where you can search for an object code. We provide instructions on searching for codes in the next lesson.

Figure 9.7 A search button (A) appears when you click inside most data entry fields.

Tip #6: Some data entry fields, and particularly date fields, are prepopulated with codes when they first appear on the screen. However, the fields are still white and in read/write mode, so you can change these default entries if necessary.

Tip #7: You can attach **selection criteria** (also called *operational conditions*) to many code fields. For instance, the code in the first **Equipment field** in Figure 9.8 is preceded by the *less than* (<) operational condition (A). Consequently, this transaction only affects equipment whose code is less than the entry (*100500*) in the field. We describe selection criteria more fully in Lesson 12.

Figure 9.8 Selection criteria (A) can be used to set conditions to coded data entries.

Tip #8: The system has a good memory: It remembers codes and texts that you entered previously in many fields. When you start to type a data entry into a field, the system searches its memory and displays a menu of matching entries. You can then use the arrow keys on your keyboard to scroll down to one of these entries, then hit the **Enter key** on your keyboard to enter it into the field.

For instance, we started to enter a work-order code in the **Order field** of the **Display Order initial screen** (Figure 9.9). As soon as we entered the first number (*2*) in this field, the system displayed all our previous order-code entries that begin with this number (A). We scrolled down to the second one with the arrow keys, then entered it in the field by hitting the **Enter key**.

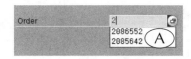

Figure 9.9 Once you start to enter code in a data entry field, the system calls up a list of previously entered codes that begin with the same characters (A).

Lesson 10
SEARCHING FOR CODES

The previous lesson provided some basic instructions on entering the codes for objects, dates, and units of measure in the data entry fields of initial screens. This next lesson answers the question: *What do I do if I don't know the codes?*

There are so many codes for so many objects in the SAP database that it is impossible to remember them all and impractical to list them all on job aids, cheat sheets, and the like. For instance, any good-sized company might well own tens of thousands of pieces of equipment, each with its own unique code, which it houses in its plants, which have their own codes. It may also stock the same number of consumable materials, each with its own code, in its warehouses, which also have their own codes.

Fortunately, SAP provides four easy-to-use popup tools for searching for codes:

- Short hit list screens
- Multiple-tab search screens
- Structure search trees
- List-display search screens

To start the process of searching for an unknown code, you simply click inside a data entry field. This action highlights that field and displays a **search button** (A) to its immediate right (Figure 10.1). Click it, and you are ready to search.

(If you are keyboard-oriented, you can alternatively click inside a data entry field to highlight it, then hit the **F4 function key** on your keyboard.)

This lesson describes the design and operation of the four search screens in the SAP system and concludes with some tips for using them effectively.

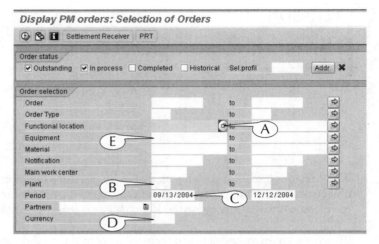

Figure 10.1   Click inside a field to call up its **search button** (A), and click it to start a search for the correct code for that field.

Short Hit List Screens

Some data entry fields can accept only a limited number of codes. When you call up and click the search buttons for these fields, a **short hit list screen** appears over the initial screen with a list of all the available codes and their descriptions. Scroll down this hit list, locate the desired code, and double-click it; the code is automatically entered in the field for you.

For instance, the **Plant field** is common to many initial screens, including the initial screen of the *IW39 transaction* (Figure 10.1B). Generally, the number of plants operated by any one company is relatively small, on the order of several to several tens. Consequently, when you click the search button for this field, you see immediately a **short hit list screen** with the names and codes of all the plants (Figure 10.2).

For this example, the short hit list screen shows the names and codes of 41 plants; this number is displayed in both the title bar at the top of this screen and the status bar at its base. Once you see this screen, scroll through the list, locate the desired plant, and double-click its name; the plant's code is automatically entered in the **Plant field** of the initial screen.

Short hit list screens appear when you search for the correct code for many objects, including bin numbers, material and movement types, priority codes, purchasing groups, and order types. They are especially common to the data entry fields of units of measure and dates.

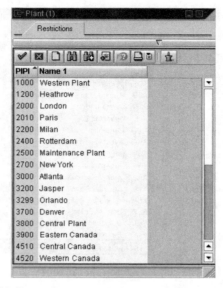

Figure 10.2   A **short hit list screen** shows all the possible codes for an object.

For example, a search for the correct code for the **Period field** on the initial screen of the *IW39 transaction* (Figure 10.1C) yields a short hit list screen with several monthly calendars (Figure 10.3). Similarly, a search for the correct code for the **Currency field** on this same screen (Figure 10.1D) yields a short hit list screen with the codes for 184 currency types (Figure 10.4).

Figure 10.3   **Short hit list screen** for dates.

Figure 10.4   Short hit list screen for currency.

Multiple-Tab Search Screens

Many data entry fields, such as the **Equipment** and **Material fields** on the initial screen of the *IW39 transaction* (Figure 10.1), could accept many hundreds or thousands of codes for objects of many different stripes and colors. When you are searching for the correct codes for these fields, the **short hit list search screen** is not a practical tool.

Consider the case of searching for the correct code for the **Equipment field** on the initial screen of the *IW39 transaction* (Figure 10.1E). When you click the search button for this field, a **multiple-tab search screen** appears over this initial screen (Figure 10.5).

The critical design elements on this search screen are its many data entry fields, which allow you to enter multiple criteria for searching for an object code. There are usually so many fields on the screens, in fact, that they are distributed throughout several subscreens, which can be displayed in one of three ways.

- Click one of the **tabs** (A) at the top of the screen.
- Click the **left** or **right control arrow** (B) to the right of the tabs to move to the next or previous subscreen in the series.
- Click the **list icon** (C) to the right of the control arrows to display a list of subscreens (D), then scroll down and click the desired one.

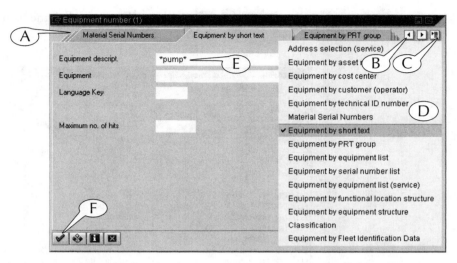

Figure 10.5   The multiple-tab search screen for the **Equipment field**. This screen is set to search for all pieces of equipment with the word *pump* in their descriptions.

You can enter one or more search criteria on any one subscreen of a multiple-tab search screen. For an example, we searched for the codes for all the pumps that are owned by a company by following this next procedure, which makes use of a single search criterion.

Procedure

Searching for a Code With a Single Search Criterion

Step 1. Locate any subscreen that contains the **Equipment descript field** (Figure 10.5E), and enter the phrase **pump**. (We explain the significance of the asterisks in the next part of this lesson.)

Step 2. Hit the **Enter key** on your keyboard, *or*

Click the **Enter button** (F) in the lower-left corner.

Step 3. The system responds with a **hit list** of equipment that matches the single search criterion (Figure 10.6). Each line of this list displays the name and the object code for one piece of equipment that has the word *pump* in its description.

We scrolled through this list, located the desired pumps, and double-clicked its line to enter its code in the **Equipment field** of the initial screen.

Note: If you do not find the desired object code on the **hit list**, you may want to return to the **multiple-tab search screen** and enter a new set of search criteria. To return to that search screen, click the bar (A) directly below the tabs on the **hit list**.

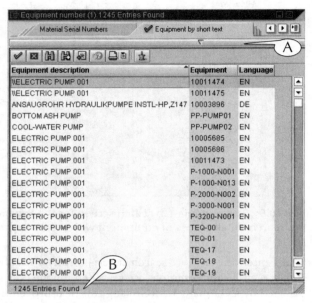

Figure 10.6   The hit list for a single-criterion search for an equipment code.

End Procedure

But what if you wanted to search for pumps that were stored at one specific plant in a company? You would follow this next procedure to search for them with these two criteria.

Procedure

Searching for a Code With Multiple Search Criteria

Step 1.   Locate a subscreen that contains the **Maintenance plant** and **Equipment descript fields** (Figure 10.7).

Step 2.   Enter the plant code in the **Maintenance plant field** (A).

Step 3.   Enter the phrase **pump** in the **Equipment descript field** (B).

Step 4.   Hit the **Enter key** on your keyboard, *or*

Click the **Enter button** (C) in the lower-left corner.

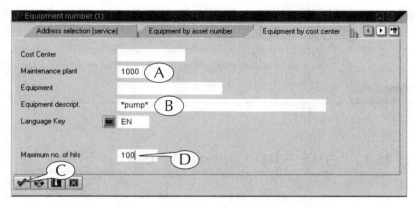

Figure 10.7   The multiple-tab search screen for the **Equipment field**. This screen is set to search for all pieces of equipment at maintenance plant 1000 with the word *pump* in their descriptions.

Step 5.   The system responds with a hit list of every piece of equipment that meets the two search criteria (Figure 10.8). Once again, each line of this hit list displays the description and code of one piece of equipment with

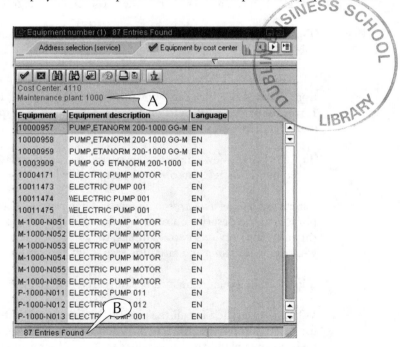

Figure 10.8   The hit list for a two-criteria search for an equipment code. The header shows that all the pumps are housed at maintenance plant 1000 (A).

the word *pump* in its description. The header of the screen shows that all these pumps are located in the specified plant (A).

Scroll through this hit list to locate the desired vehicle and double-click its line to enter its code in the **Equipment field** of the initial screen.

End Procedure

Tips for Using Multiple-Tab Search Screens

We are going to draw upon these examples of searches for equipment codes to discuss some general tips for using multiple-tab search screens.

Tip #1: When you click the **search button** for any data entry field to call up its multiple-tab search screen, the subscreen that appears will be the last one you used when you searched for this same datatype code.

The system has a good memory for your preferences in search screens (and other things). You can always change the subscreen by clicking another tab, however.

Tip #2: Entry fields for the most useful search criteria appear on nearly every subscreen.

The most commonly used search criterion for equipment codes is their description. (This is also true for many other objects.) Consequently, you will find the **Equipment descript field** on every subscreen of the equipment multiple-tab search screen.

Tip #3: Enter a few characters or partial words or phrases, preceded and followed by asterisks (*), in object description fields.

Asterisks serve as *wildcards* in a search: They represent any characters, words, or phrases in the description of an object other than the exact content between them. In the previous two examples, they trigger a search for any equipment with the word *pump* and anything else in its description.

Tip #4: The greater the number of search criteria, the shorter the hit list.

When we searched for all the pumps in our company, the hit list displayed data for 1,245 pumps (Figure 10.6B). When we restricted this search to pumps in one maintenance plant, the hit list displayed data for 87 pumps (Figure 10.8B).

The same rule applies for an entry in an object description field: the longer it is, the shorter the hit list. For instance, if we had entered *pump, etanorm* in the **Equipment descript field** during our two searches, the hit lists would have been considerably shorter, for very few pumps have that phrase in their description.

But *too short* an entry in an object description field is not a good thing either. For instance, if we had entered *p* in the **Equipment descript field** during our example searches, the hit lists would have been ridiculously long, because they would have displayed the data for every piece of equipment with the letter *p* in its description.

Tip #5: Don't assume that descriptions are spelled out, or spelled correctly.

Suppose you want to search for the code for an electrical transformer. You may be inclined to enter *transformer* in the **Equipment descript field**, but you would be making a mistake: Utility workers use the jargon *xformer* to describe this sort of equipment.

Similarly, suppose you want to search for the code for electrical conductor (that is, wire). You may be inclined to enter *conductor* in the **Equipment descript field**. You are assuming that everyone (including the folks who configured SAP for your company) knows how to spell this word correctly (they might misspell it *conducter*).

And of course, you must watch out for regional differences in spelling. The most obvious example is the spelling of *colour* by British speakers of the English language versus its spelling as *color* by American speakers of English. When you are dealing with two people separated by a common tongue, such discrepancies can happen frequently.

Tip #6: Consider the possible number of hits you might get in a search, and set up the search screen accordingly.

Every subscreen of every multiple-tab search screen contains a field called **Maximum no of hits** (see Figure 10.7D). This field contains a default value—in our case, *100*—that restricts the contents of the hit list to the first 100 objects that meet your selection criteria. If the search finds more than 100 objects that match your criteria, it displays only these first 100 matches and posts a message in its status bar that reads *More than 100 input options* (Figure 10.9A).

When this happens, you must return to the search screen, delete the entry in the **Maximum no of hits field** and execute the search again. Save yourself the extra work and delete this entry before you conduct a search if you suspect there might be more than 100 hits.

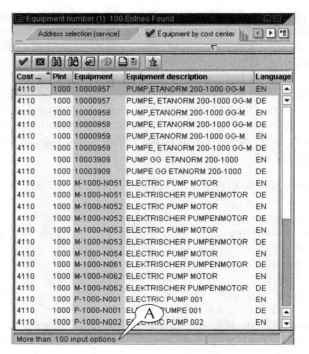

Figure 10.9   The hit list tells you with a message in its status bar (A) that more than 100 objects matched your search criteria.

Tip #7: You can attach operational conditions (called *selection options*) such as *greater than* (>) or *less than* (<) to any data entry field by double-clicking inside it and selecting the condition from a popup screen.

See Lesson 12 for more instructions on using selection options.

Tip #8: Search hit lists display their output in the order of the object code by default. For example, a hit list for equipment displays the matching objects in the order of the equipment code (Figure 10.10). This makes it difficult to locate a specific piece of equipment on the hit list by its description, because the column for the equipment code datatype (with the header *Equipment description*) is randomly ordered.

However, you can sort a hit list according to the contents of any column by clicking that column's header. For instance, one click of the header of the **Equipment description column** (Figure 10.10A) sorts the hit list in alphabetical order (Figure 10.11), and a second click sorts it in reverse order.

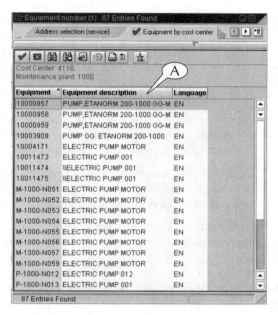

Figure 10.10   This hit list for an equipment search displays its output in the order of the equipment code.

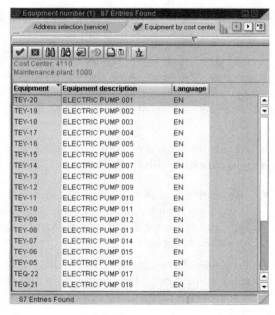

Figure 10.11   Click the header of the **Equipment description column** to reorganize this hit list in the order of that datatype.

Structure Search Tree

There may be circumstances in which you are searching for the correct code for an object that is part of a larger hierarchy of objects. Some objects that fall into this category include the following.

- Personnel in a company or an organization: for example, personnel organized in a hierarchy of president, vice presidents, managers, assistant managers, administrative assistants, and so on down

- Equipment in an assemblage of functionally related equipment: for example, a transformer that is part of a neighborhood power substation, which is part of a regional electrical generation and distribution system

- Organizational units in a business: for example, a department within a business unit within a regional office of a global corporation

When this case arises, you might find a **Structure search tab** (Figure 10.12A) on the multiple-tab search screen for the object. Click it, and the search screen is replaced by a *multilevel structure tree* (Figure 10.13).

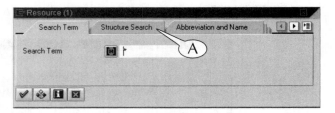

Figure 10.12   Click the **Structure Search tab** (A) on a multiple-tab search screen to display a structure search tree for organizational units.

Structure search trees are very similar in their design and operation to **menu folders** and **Favorites folders** (see Lessons 5 and 6). For example:

- First-level "branches" in a structure tree identify the major classes of the object. For example, the first-level branches in Figure 10.13 identify the key business groups in a corporation, including *Sales UK*, *Accounting*, *Avanex*, and *Bose* (A).

- Second-level branches identify subdivisions of the major classes. For example, the second-level branches in Figure 10.13 identify departments *Automotive Products* and *Home Entertainment* (B) within the *Bose* business group.

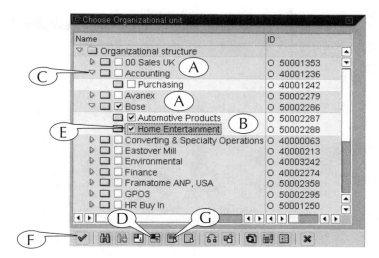

Figure 10.13 A structure search tree for organizational units.

You can expand the branches in a structure tree to display their upper-level branches in one of three ways.

- Click the **control arrow** (C) to the left of a specific branch name to reveal the next set of branches beneath it, *or*

  Double-click a branch name to reveal the next set of branches beneath it, *or*

  Click the **Expand all button** (D) to expand all the branches in the structure tree. This is the least optimal method, because it takes some time for the system to display all the branches in the structure tree.

You can select one or more objects in the structure tree by clicking their selection boxes to place checks inside them (E), then clicking the **Enter button** (F) to enter them in a data entry field. If you select multiple objects, they are automatically entered on the multiple selection screen for a field.

You can also select all the objects in one level of the structure tree—for example, both departments in the *Bose* business group—by selecting the lower-level branch above it (*Bose*), then clicking the **Select all button** (G).

You may also encounter a simpler structure search tree when you search for the correct codes for certain objects. For example, when you trigger a search for the correct code to describe structural damages to equipment, the system automatically displays a structure search tree with folder icons (A) in place of the control arrows (Figure 10.14). You would then open its folders and subfolders to locate the correct code by clicking the icons once, then double-click the desired code to enter it in the data field in question.

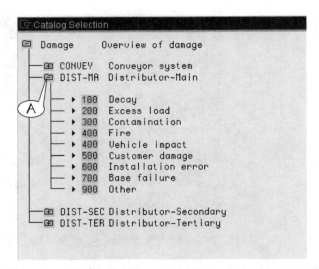

Figure 10.14   A simple structure search tree with folder and subfolder icons.

List-Display Search Screens

When you click some tabs on a multiple-tab search screen, this screen is erased and replaced by a full-sized screen with many entry fields for your search criteria. This screen is actually identical to the initial screens of *list-display transactions* (which we discuss at the end of this book), but it can be used for searches in the exact same manner as the smaller subscreens of a multiple-tab search screen.

For example, the multiple-tab search screen for equipment codes contains a tab called **Equipment by equipment list**. When you click it, this search screen is replaced by the **Display Equipment: Equipment Selection screen**, a much larger search screen with many data entry fields (Figure 10.15). Despite its size, however, you can use this **list-display search screen** as you would any sub-screen of the multiple-tab search screen: Enter one or more search criteria in the available fields, and then click the **Execute button** (A) to execute the search and display a hit list.

Suppose you call up this **list-display search screen** and then decide to use another subscreen of the multiple-tab search screen. How do you get back to that search screen?

Simple: Click the **Back button** (B) in the standard toolbar of the **list-display search screen** to call up the **Selection of Input Help popup screen** (Figure 10.16). This screen contains a list of the other available subscreens of that multiple-tab search screen. Double-click the desired one, and it appears.

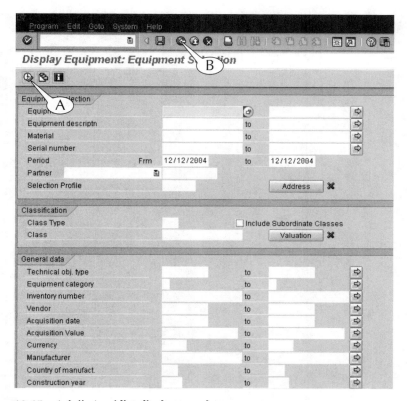

Figure 10.15   A full-sized **list-display search screen**.

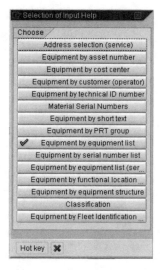

Figure 10.16   A menu of subscreens for the multiple-tab search screen for equipment codes.

Lesson 11

ENTERING CODES ON MULTIPLE SELECTION SCREENS

The first two lessons of this part of this book provided instructions on searching for and entering single codes and data values, or ranges of codes and data values, in the **data entry fields** of initial screens.

Now consider this scenario. You are a warehouse manager, and you want to generate a report on the available stock of about 100 different consumable materials at your warehouse. Some of these materials have randomly numbered, nonconsecutive object codes (called *material numbers* or *material codes*), and some have consecutively numbered material codes that fall within three different ranges.

To acquire this data, you would execute the *MM60 transaction*, which reports the stock levels and storage locations of materials. You would navigate to the initial screen of the transaction (Figure 11.1), enter the codes for the materials in question in the **Material fields** (A) and the warehouse code in the **Plant field** (B), then click the **Execute button** (C) to generate the report.

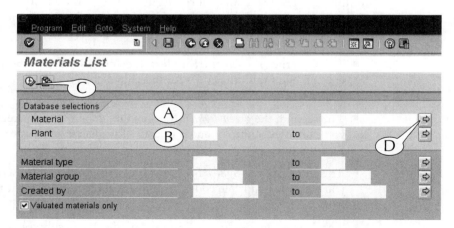

Figure 11.1 The initial screen of the *MM60 transaction*, with the **Material fields** (A) and its accompanying **Multiple selection button** (D).

However, the initial screen for the *MM60 transaction* contains only one set of paired **Material fields**, in which you can enter either one material code or one range of codes. There is no place on this screen for entering the codes for all 100 materials on which you want to report.

Of course, you could simply execute this transaction several times, each time entering a different single material code or range of codes in the **Material fields**. However, you can also enter multiple nonconsecutive codes and multiple ranges of codes with the **multiple selection screen** for these fields, which you can call up by clicking the **Multiple selection button** (D) to their immediate right.

This lesson provides instructions on using the **multiple selection screen**. We use this example of reporting material stocks to illustrate these instructions, but be assured that this screen is exactly the same in its design and operation for all data entry fields on all initial screens.

Design and Operation of a Multiple Selection Screen

The **Multiple Selection for Material screen** (Figure 11.2) displays four subscreens, which you call up by clicking their tabs (A). (We show two of these subscreens in the figure.) Each subscreen contains either one column of single data entry fields or two columns of paired fields, wherein you enter the codes for the object in question. The bottom of the screen contains a row of **buttons** (B), which you use to work with the contents of the screen.

The tabs of a multiple selection screen are color-coded—the first two contain a **green light**, the last two contain a **red light**—and are named either *Single vals* (that is, *values*) or *Ranges*. This combination of color and name defines the different functions of the subscreens.

- The first, the *green-lighted* **Single values tab**, displays a subscreen where you can enter multiple codes for individual objects you want to *include* in a transaction.

- The second, the *green-lighted* **Ranges tab**, displays a subscreen where you can enter multiple ranges of codes for objects you want to *include* in a transaction.

- The third, the *red-lighted* **Single values tab**, displays a subscreen where you can enter multiple codes for individual objects you want to *exclude* from a transaction.

- The fourth, the *red-lighted* **Ranges tab**, displays a subscreen where you can enter multiple ranges of codes for objects you want to *exclude* from a transaction.

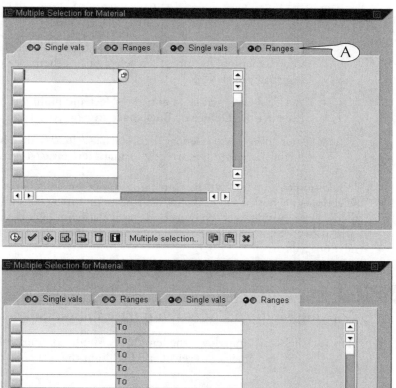

Figure 11.2   Two of the four subscreens of the **Multiple Selection for Material** screen for equipment codes.

You enter codes in the data entry fields of the multiple selection screen in the same manner as you enter them on an initial screen.

- Click inside a field to select and highlight it, and then type your entry on your keyboard.

- Copy data from another source into your clipboard, then click inside a field on the multiple selection screen and hit the keystroke **Ctrl + V** to paste the data there.

- Search for the correct code for a field by clicking inside it to call up its search button, then clicking it to start the search.

- Apply selection options to a single field by double-clicking inside it to call up a menu of options, then select one of them (see the next lesson for instructions).

- Click-and-drag across an entry to select and highlight it, then delete it by hitting the **Delete** or **Backspace key** on your keyboard.

- Enter abbreviated calendar dates (such as *010104*), then hit the **Enter key** on your keyboard to correctly format them (as *01/01/2004* in this case).

In addition to copying-and-pasting a single code into a field on the multiple selection screen, you can also copy-and-paste multiple codes into a column of fields. For example, you can copy-and-paste a column of codes from an *Excel* spreadsheet (Figure 11.3) onto the multiple selection screen by following this next procedure.

Procedure

Copying Multiple Codes Onto the Multiple Selection Screen

Step 1. Click-and-drag down the length of a single column of data cells on the Excel spreadsheet to select and highlight them (Figure 11.3A).

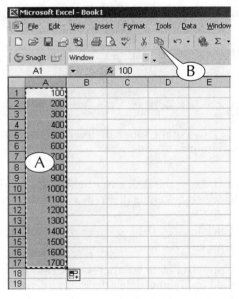

Figure 11.3 Copying a column of data from an *Excel* spreadsheet into your computer's clipboard.

Step 2. Copy the data into your clipboard by clicking the **Copy button** (B), *or* Hit the keystroke **Ctrl + C**.

Step 3. Click inside the first available field (Figure 11.4A) in a single column of data entry fields on the **Multiple Selection for Material screen**.

Step 4. Hit the keystroke **Ctrl + V** to paste the data from your clipboard into the column. The system automatically adds any additional fields that are needed to fit all the copied data onto the screen.

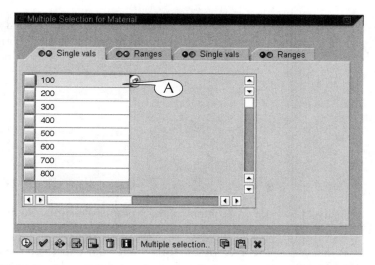

Figure 11.4   Pasting copied data from the clipboard to the **Multiple Selection for Material screen**.

End Procedure

A multiple selection screen has a row of buttons at its bottom for working with its contents (Figure 11.5). The functions of some of these buttons, most notably the **Enter, Selection options**, **Delete selection** (that is, delete a line), and **Paste from clipboard buttons,** are executed more efficiently by the methods that were described above, so we do not describe them here.

The most important button on the multiple selection screen is **Copy**. Once you complete all your entries on the screen, you must click the **Copy button** to save your entries and return to the initial screen.

The other useful buttons at the bottom of the multiple selection screen are

- **Insert line**, which adds another single field or set of paired fields to a subscreen;

- **Delete all**, which deletes the contents in all the fields on all the subscreens;

- **Multiple selection**, which allows you to search for and enter multiple codes in one fell swoop on a subscreen (and which we describe at the end of this lesson);

- **Cancel**, which terminates the setup of the screen and returns you to the initial screen. (A control button in the upper-right corner also serves this purpose.)

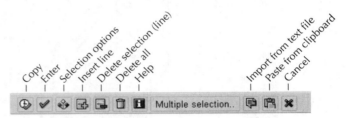

Figure 11.5   The tool buttons of the multiple selection screen.

When you click the **Copy button** to save your entries on the multiple selection screen, the screen is erased and you can complete the setup of the initial screen of the transaction. However, you will notice a change to the fields in which you entered the multiple codes (Figure 11.6).

- If you entered multiple codes on the green-lighted Single values subscreen, the first of those codes appears in the first of the two paired fields (A) and the Multiple Selection button is highlighted with a green rectangle (B).

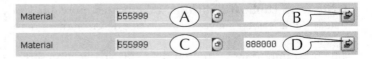

Figure 11.6   The first entries on the multiple selection screen appear in the datatype fields, and the Multiple selection button (B and D) is highlighted to indicate that codes have been entered on that screen.

- If you entered multiple ranges of codes on the green-lighted Ranges subscreen, the first of those ranges appears in the paired fields (C) and the Multiple Selection button is highlighted with a green rectangle (D).

At this point, you can always recall the multiple selection screen and edit its contents by clicking the **Multiple selection button** again. Once there, add, edit, or delete the codes, then click the **Copy button** to save your changes and return to the initial screen.

Using the Multiple Selection Screen: An Example

Let's return to the scenario described at the start of this lesson. A warehouse manager wants to create a report of the available stock of 100 consumable materials by executing the *MM60 transaction*. The object codes for these materials are given in Table 11.1.

Table 11.1   Object codes for the scenario

Report on these materials	Exceptions to ranges
100500	
361010	
410885	
638477	
914242	
200600-200620	*but not* 200615 and 200617
564400-564425	*but not* 564411 through 564417
711015-711115	*but not* 711035 through 711075

The manager would follow these steps to report the stock levels on all these materials in one transaction.

Step 1. Click the **Multiple selection button** for the **Material field** (Figure 11.1D) to call up its multiple selection screen.

Step 2. Click the green-lighted **Single vals tab**, and enter the five single codes in the left column of Table 11.1 in the first five single fields (Figure 11.7). This sets up the transaction to report the stock data for these five materials.

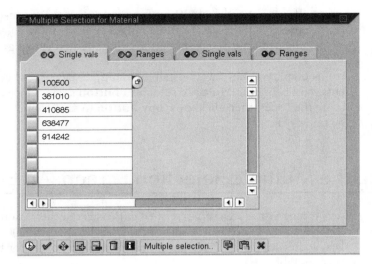

Figure 11.7   Five object codes are entered on this green-lighted subscreen. The objects will be included in the output report of the *MM60 transaction*.

Step 3.   Click the green-lighted **Ranges tab**, and enter the three ranges of codes in the left column of Table 11.1 in the first three paired fields (Figure 11.8). This sets up the transaction to report the stock data for all the materials with codes within these three ranges.

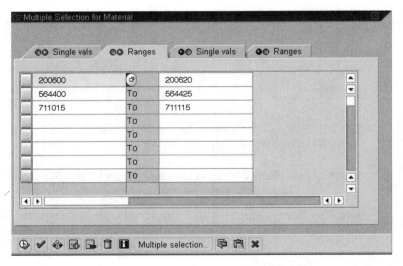

Figure 11.8   Three ranges of object codes are entered on this green-lighted subscreen. The objects with codes within these ranges will be included in the output report of the *MM60 transaction*.

Step 4. Click the red-lighted **Single vals tab,** and enter the two exceptional single codes in the right column of the table in the first two single fields (Figure 11.9). This sets up the transaction to exclude these two materials from the report.

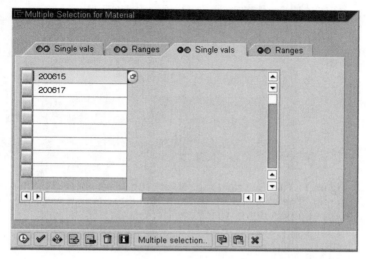

Figure 11.9 Two object codes are entered on this red-lighted subscreen. The objects will be excluded from the output report of the *MM60 transaction.*

Step 5. Click the red-lighted **Ranges tab,** and enter the two exceptional ranges of codes in the right column of the table in the first two open range fields (Figure 11.10). This sets up the transaction to exclude all materials with codes within these two ranges from the report.

Step 6. Click the **Copy button** at the bottom of the **Multiple Selection for Material screen** (Figure 11.10A) to save the entries and return to the initial screen.

Step 7. Continue the setup of the initial screen, then execute the transaction.

This is a fairly complex example of the use of a multiple selection screen, in that it uses all four subscreens to enter codes for objects to be included and excluded from the transaction. Generally, you might use one or two of the subscreens, not all four. We used this example to demonstrate that it is a relatively simple task to set up the screen for even such a complex task, and a great time saver to boot.

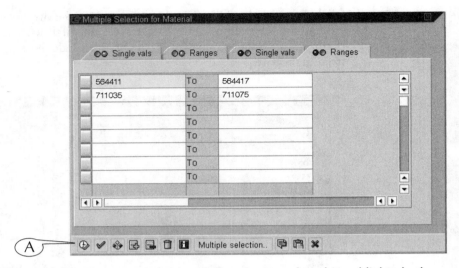

Figure 11.10   Two ranges of object codes are entered on this red-lighted sub-screen. The objects with codes within these ranges will be excluded from the output report of the *MM60 transaction*.

Using the Multiple Selection Button

We have already mentioned that you can search for the correct code for any field on the multiple selection screen in the usual manner: Simply click inside the field to call up its search button, click it, then follow the instructions in the previous lesson.

This process enables you to search for and enter a *single* code for a field. However, you can also search for and enter *multiple* codes on the multiple search screen by using the **Multiple selection button** at its bottom.

To illustrate this, we search for the codes for several pumps by following this next procedure. This procedure begins after the multiple selection screen for the **Equipment field** of an initial screen has been called up.

<h2 style="background:black;color:white;display:inline-block">Procedure</h2>

Searching for Multiple Codes for the Multiple Selection Screen

Step 1. Click the green-lighted **Single vals tab** (A) on the multiple selection screen (Figure 11.11). (*Note:* This procedure works only on the single-value subscreens of the screen.)

Step 2. Click the **Multiple selection button** at the bottom of this screen (B).

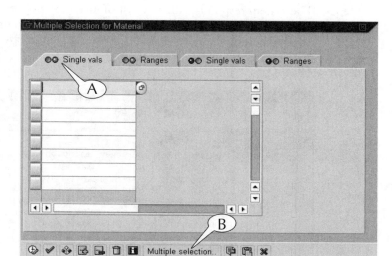

Figure 11.11 The first two steps in searching for multiple codes for the multiple selection screen.

Step 3. The **multiple-tab search screen** for equipment codes appears (Figure 11.12). Enter search criteria on the appropriate subscreen. For this example, we entered *1000* in the **Maintenance plant field** (A) and **pump** in the **Equipment descript field** (B).

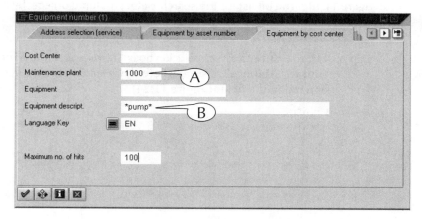

Figure 11.12 Search criteria are entered on the **multiple-tab search screen**.

Step 4. Hit the **Enter key** on your keyboard to conduct the search.

Step 5. The system responds with a hit list of matching objects (Figure 11.13). Notice that each line of the list has a selection box on its left end (A). Select the desired objects by clicking their selection boxes to place check marks inside them.

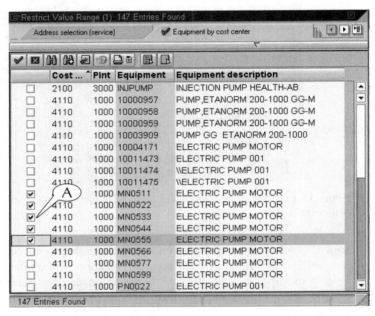

Figure 11.13   The hit list for the search. Select multiple objects by clicking their selection boxes (A).

Step 6. Hit the **Enter key** on your keyboard to return to the **Multiple Selection for Material screen**, where the selected object codes are now entered in the fields (Figure 11.14).

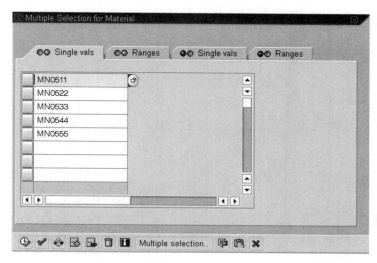

Figure 11.14   The codes for the objects selected in Figure 11.13 are entered on the **Multiple Selection for Material screen.**

End Procedure

Lesson 12

USING SELECTION OPTIONS ON DATA ENTRY FIELDS

This lesson describes the procedure for attaching **selection options** to data entry fields on initial screens, search screens, and multiple selection screens.

Selection options are *conditional indicators* that mark the limits of the codes in data entry fields. To explain this definition, we offer two examples from the initial screen of the *IW29 transaction*, which displays a list of notifications[1] for a maintenance-plant manager.

For our first example, we set up the initial screen of the *IW29 transaction* to generate a list of all *completed notifications* for equipment *100500* that were created in *2004* by doing the following (Figure 12.1):

- We selected the *Completed option* (A) in the **Notification status field area**.

- We entered the object code *100500* in the first of the two **Equipment fields** (B).

- We entered *01/01/2004* and *12/31/2004* in the **Created on fields** (C).

---

1. A notification is a record in the SAP database that equipment needs maintenance work because it is malfunctioning or not operating at its optimal level.

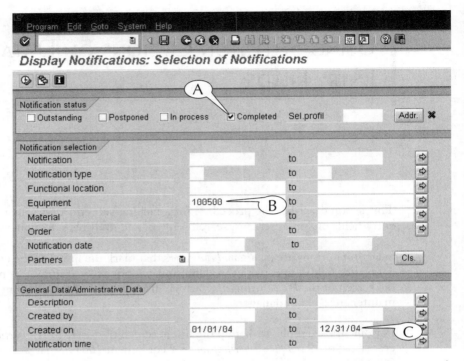

Figure 12.1   The initial screen of the IW29 transaction, set up for the first example.

For our second example, we set up the initial screen to generate a list of all *completed notifications* for equipment *100500* that were created *before* the year 2004 by doing the following (Figure 12.2):

- We again selected the *Completed option* (A) in the **Notification status field area**.

- We again entered the object code *100500* in the first of the two **Equipment fields** (B).

- We entered *01/01/2004* in the first of the two **Created on fields**, then attached the *green less than selection option* to the field. This option is indicated by the less than (<) symbol to the left of the field (C). This entry alerts the system that there is a condition to the transaction: We want to generate a list of only those notifications with dates less than—that is, prior to—January 1, 2004.

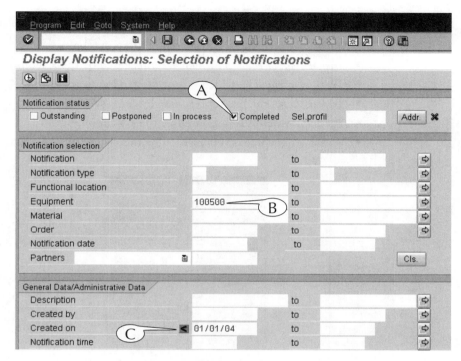

Figure 12.2   The initial screen of the IW29 transaction, set up for the second example, which includes a selection option on the **Created on field**.

Attaching Selection Options to Data Entry Fields

You can attach selection options to many data entry fields on many initial screens, as well as those on search screens and multiple selection screens. You select the desired option from the **Maintain Selection Options popup screen**, which you call up by double-clicking inside a data entry field.

The **Maintain Selection Options screen** displays a menu of six *green-colored* selection options by default (Figure 12.3). It also has two menu buttons directly below this menu (A):

- **Select**, which displays the menu of green selection options

- **Exclude from selection**, which displays an alternative menu of six *red-colored* selection options on the **Exclude Initial Value from Selection screen** (Figure 12.4)

Both menus contain six selection options:

- *Single value*, which is represented by the = symbol
- *Greater than or equal to*, which is represented by the ≥ symbol
- *Less than or equal to*, which is represented by the ≤ symbol
- *Greater than*, which is represented by the > symbol
- *Less than*, which is represented by the < symbol
- *Not equal to*, which is represented by the ≠ symbol

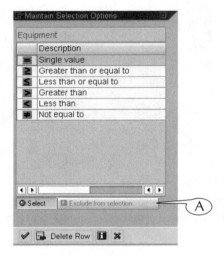

Figure 12.3   The green selection options menu.

Figure 12.4   The red selection options menu.

Procedure

Attaching a Selection Option to a Data Entry Field

Step 1. Double-click inside the field to call up the **Maintain Selection Options screen**.

Step 2. Select either the red or green menu with the menu buttons (Figure 12.3A).

Step 3. Double-click a selection option in the menu. The **Maintain Selection Options screen** is erased, and the symbol for the selected option is added to the data entry field on the initial screen.

End Procedure

Procedure

Removing a Selection Option From a Data Entry Field

Step 1. Double-click inside the field to call up the **Maintain Selection Options screen**.

Step 2. Click the **Delete row button** (e.g., Figure 12.4A) at the bottom of the screen.

Step 3. Hit the **Enter key** on the keyboard to save your change.

End Procedure

Which is green and which is red?

The symbols for selection options are colored green and red, but you can't see these colors in this book. We describe the green and red selection options under different headers of this lesson so that you won't get them confused.

However, you can also tell them apart by the font colors: the green symbols appear in a black-colored font against the background, and the red symbols appear in a white-colored font against the background.

What Do the Green Selection Options Do?

We attach green selection options to the **Equipment fields** of the initial screen of the *IW29 transaction* to explain and illustrate their functions.

The *green single value selection option* causes this transaction to impact only the object whose code is entered in the first **Equipment field**. For example, the initial screen in Figure 12.5 is set to generate a list of notifications for only the single piece of equipment with the object code *100500*.

Figure 12.5   Using the green single value selection option.

There is really no purpose to attaching this selection option to any data entry field, because it is implicit that any transaction impacts the objects whose codes are entered in the fields of its initial screen. Nonetheless, you will find that it is automatically attached to some fields, particularly on **search screens** and **multiple selection screens** (for example, Figure 12.6A).

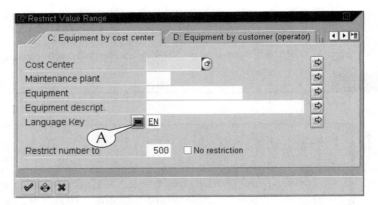

Figure 12.6   Selection options are commonly entered automatically on search screens.

The *green greater than or equal to selection option* causes this transaction to impact only those objects whose code is equal to or greater than the code in the first **Equipment field**. For example, the initial screen in Figure 12.7 is set to generate a list of notifications for all equipment with the object codes *100500* and higher.

Figure 12.7 Using the green greater than or equal to selection option.

The *green less than or equal to selection option* causes this transaction to impact only those objects whose code is equal to or less than the code in the first **Equipment field**. For example, the initial screen in Figure 12.8 is set to generate a list of notifications for all equipment with the object code *100500* and lower.

Figure 12.8 Using the green less than or equal to selection option.

The *green greater than selection option* causes this transaction to impact only those objects whose code is greater than the code in the first **Equipment field**, but *not* the object with that code. For example, the initial screen in Figure 12.9 is set to generate a list of notifications for all equipment with object codes greater than *100500*, but *not* the equipment with that same code.

Figure 12.9 Using the green greater than selection option.

The *green less than selection option* causes this transaction to impact only those objects whose code is less than the code in the first **Equipment field**, but *not* the object with that code. For example, the initial screen in Figure 12.10 is set to generate a list of notifications for all equipment with object codes less than *100500*, but *not* the equipment with that same code.

Figure 12.10 Using the green less than selection option.

The *green not equal to selection option* causes the transaction to exclude the object whose code is entered in a field.

We don't recommend using this selection option on any initial or search screen: If you don't want to include an object in a transaction, *don't enter its code on the screen*. We also don't recommend its use on multiple selection screens, where you have two red-lighted subscreens for entering the codes of objects to be excluded from a transaction.

What Do the Red Selection Options Do?

The red selection options have exactly the opposite impact of the green ones.

For example, the *red greater than or equal to selection option* causes the transaction to ignore those objects whose code is equal to or greater than the code in a data entry field. For example, the initial screen in Figure 12.11 is set to ignore the notifications for all equipment with object codes *100500* and higher.

Figure 12.11   Using the red greater than or equal to selection option (if you must).

Once again, we don't recommend the use of the red selection options on most screens for the same reason that we don't recommend the use of the *green not equal to selection option*. The exception to this generalization is filter screens, which are discussed in Lesson 14.

Lesson 13
WORKING WITH SCREEN VARIANTS

We discussed the different methods for entering data on the initial screens of transactions in the previous lessons in this part of our book. We now close this part with a discussion of **screen variants**.

Screen variants are customized versions of initial screens. When SAP is implemented by your SAP administrators, there is always some customization or *configuration* work performed on the initial screens by computer developers so that the default versions of these screens address the needs and practices of your company. For example, they might program the system to show selected data entry fields on initial screens; to hide the fields for data that are not collected by your company; or to automatically enter default values (such as company codes or dates) in some fields.

However, you can further customize some of the initial screens that you regularly use so that you can work with them more easily and efficiently. Specifically, you can

- Add data entry fields that are not present on the default versions of initial screens, but which you might need for your work;

- Create default values for data entry fields in which you always enter the same content;

- Hide data entry fields that you do not need for your work but that are present on the default versions of initial screens;

- Save your customized screens so that they appear automatically when you call them up in the future.

This lesson provides instructions for customizing your initial screens in these ways.

Adding Data Entry Fields With the Dynamic Selections Button

List-display transactions are one of the four basic SAP transaction types (which we describe at the end of this book). Generally, they are used to create lists of related objects, such as:

- Equipment operated and maintained by a physical plant
- Purchase requisitions created by a purchasing agent
- Employees working in a business department

The initial screens of list-display transactions usually contain several data entry fields in which you enter one or several **selection criteria** and thereby define the relationship between the objects in question.

For an example, consider the initial screen for the *CJI3 list-display transaction* (Figure 13.1). This transaction generates a **line-item cost report** (which is a list of actual expenses) for construction and maintenance projects. It contains three field areas in which you define the relationship between the costs you want to see in the cost report:

- The **Project Management Selections field area**, in which you enter the codes for one or more projects or one or more components of a project (known as *WBS elements*)

- The **Cost Elements field area**, in which you enter the codes for one or more cost categories (called *cost elements*) such as salaries, travel, and medical costs, or the code for a **cost element group** (a set of cost categories)

- The **Posting Data field area**, in which you enter dates to limit the report to costs that were charged during certain time periods

We set up the initial screen in Figure 13.1 by entering the code for a project in the first of the two **Project fields** (A); the code for the salary cost element in the first of the two **Cost Element fields** (B); and a range of dates in the **Posting date fields** (C). The output of the transaction will then list costs that meet those three selection criteria: that is, all salary costs to that project during that time period, and only those costs.

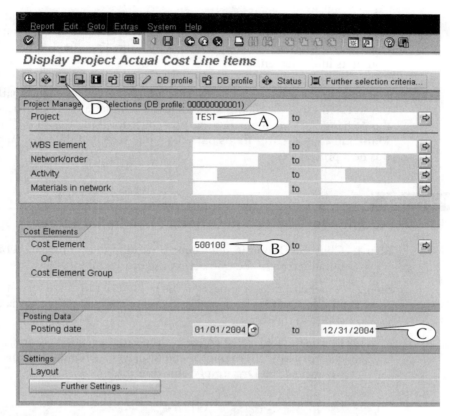

Figure 13.1   The initial screen for the *CJI3 transaction.*

Now suppose you want to limit the output of this report even further in these two ways.

- First, you want to limit it to the salary costs for the construction workers who operate out of *one of several physical plants* in your company.

- Second, you want to limit it to the construction workers in *one department* (called a *cost center*) in that physical plant, for example, the Electrical Installation department.

For this purpose, you must enter the codes for the physical plant and department in question in the **Plant** and **Cost Center fields**—except there are no such fields on the initial screen.

Why not? When SAP was first implemented by your SAP administrator, the computer developers probably did not anticipate that you might want to use this transaction in this way, so they didn't include these two fields on the default version of its initial screen.

Fortunately, the folks at SAP know that business practices change with time, so they created a tool for adding selection criteria to initial screens to accommodate those changes. We demonstrate the procedure for using this tool by adding the **Plant** and **Cost Center fields** onto the initial screen of the *CJI3 transaction* in this next procedure.

Procedure

Adding More Selection Criteria to an Initial Screen

Step 1.   Click the **Dynamic selections button** in the application toolbar of the initial screen of the transaction (Figure 13.1D).

Step 2.   A menu of folders appears at the top left of the initial screen (Figure 13.2A). Each folder contains several related selection criteria that can be added to the screen.

Locate the folder that contains the desired selection criteria, and click its control arrow (B) to open it and display its contents. For this example, we opened the **Org units definition folder**.

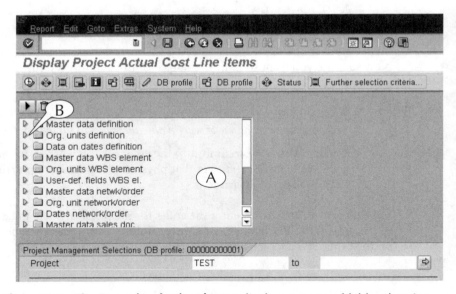

Figure 13.2   The **Dynamic selections button** displays a menu of folders bearing additional selection criteria. Click their control arrows to open them.

Step 3. Scroll down the list of selection criteria in the folder (Figure 13.3A), and double-click the desired ones. For this example, we double-clicked **Plant** and **Cost Center**.

Step 4. The **Dynamic selections field area** appears at the top right of the initial screen with data entry fields for the new selection criteria (Figure 13.3B).

Note: These new fields are fully functional. You can search for the correct code for them in the usual manner, and you can enter multiple codes by using the multiple selection buttons to their right.

You can delete any new field by clicking its name once in the menu to select and highlight it, then clicking the **Delete button** (C).

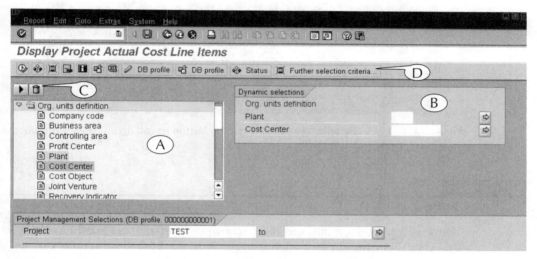

Figure 13.3   Double-click selection criteria in the menu (A), and they appear on the screen (B).

Step 5. If you cannot find the selection criteria you need in this menu, click the **Further selection criteria button** (D) in the application toolbar of the initial screen, and a second popup screen, the **Define More Selection Criteria screen,** appears with more folders bearing even more selection criteria (Figure 13.4).

- Follow Steps 3 and 4 to select additional selection criteria and display their data entry fields on the **Define More Selection Criteria screen**. For this example, we opened the **Organizational units folder** and from it added the **Company Code** and **Business Area fields** (Figure 13.4A).

- Enter codes in these additional data entry fields.

- Click the **Save button** (B) to save these entries and return to the initial screen.

Step 6. Complete the initial screen by entering codes in all the necessary data entry fields, including the two new ones, and execute the transaction.

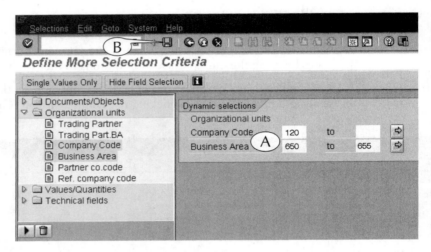

Figure 13.4   Click the **Further selection criteria button** to call up a screen with more selection criteria.

End Procedure

We should point out that some initial screens contain only the **Further selection criteria button** in their application toolbar. For instance, this is the case for the initial screen of the *KSB1 transaction* (Figure 13.5), which creates a line-item cost report for a department (called a *cost center*) in a business or an organization.

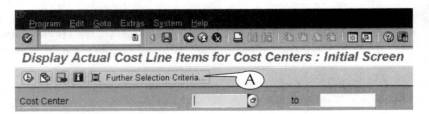

Figure 13.5   Some initial screens, like this one for the *KSB1 transaction*, have only one tool in their application toolbar for displaying additional selection criteria options.

When you click this button (A), you do not get an on-screen menu of folders and selection criteria; rather, the **Define More Selection Criteria screen** pops up over the initial screen with these objects (Figure 13.6). Once again, follow the instructions in Step 5 to add more selection criteria to the initial screen of the transaction.

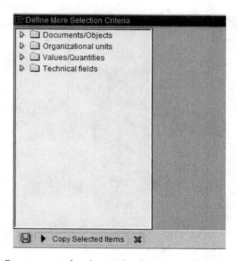

Figure 13.6   The **Define More Selection Criteria screen** for the initial screen of the *KSB1 transaction.*

Creating Screen Variants

We now demonstrate the procedure for creating and saving screen variants. This procedure can be used on all initial screens, but for an example, we create a variant for the initial screen of the *ME5A list-display transaction* (Figure 13.7). This transaction creates a list of related requisitions for the purchase of materials.

This initial screen contains many data entry fields and selection boxes for defining the selection criteria for the output report. We set up our initial screen, for instance, as follows.

- We enter the code for the purchasing agent who handles requisitions for our department in the **Purchasing group field** (A) so that the report only lists the requisitions for our department.

- We enter the code for our work location in the **Plant field** (B) so that the report is limited to materials that are delivered there, rather than to another office of our department in another state.

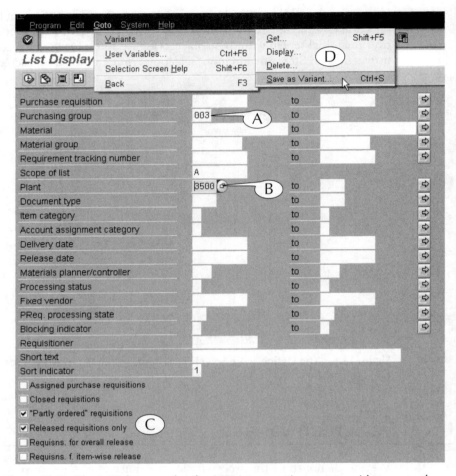

Figure 13.7   The initial screen for the *ME5A transaction*, set up with our usual choices of selection criteria and showing the menu path for creating a screen variant.

- We select the *Partly ordered requisitions* and *Released requisitions only options* (C) so that the report is limited to materials that have not been delivered.

We always make these same three entries and selections whenever we run this transaction, because they always yield a list of all our requisitions. Sometimes, however, we cut down the length of this list by adding more selection criteria in other fields. For example, when we want to limit the list to the requisitions for a specific material, we enter its code in the **Material field**; when we want to limit the list to materials from a specific source, we enter a vendor code in the **Fixed vendor field**; and so on.

By the same token, we never enter selection criteria in many other fields, including the **Document type**, **Release date**, **Order**, and **Materials planner/ controller fields**, because we do not track these data in our work (though users in other departments do). In addition, we never select the *Assigned purchase requisitions option* (we don't assign requisitions in our company) or *Closed requisitions option* (we are not interested in completed requisitions).

Given the way that we use this transaction, we created a customized variant of its initial screen by following the steps in this next procedure.

Procedure

Creating a Variant of an Initial Screen

Step 1. Navigate to the default initial screen of the transaction.

Step 2. Enter those data and select those options that you want to have prepopulated on the initial screen variant when you navigate to it. We entered codes and text in the **Purchasing group** and **Plant fields** and selected the two of the requisition type options (Figure 13.7A–C).

Step 3. Follow the menu path **Goto > Variants > Save as Variant** (Figure 13.7D), *or*

Hit the keystroke **Ctrl + S**, *or*

Click the **Save button** in the standard toolbar.

Step 4. The **ABAP: Save as Variant screen** appears (Figure 13.8). Enter a name for your variant in the **Variant name field** (A). You have two options here.

- To create a *temporary* variant, give it any name. When you return to the initial screen, this variant appears. However, if you navigate to another screen or log off and then return to the initial screen later, the default version will appear. If you want to use your screen variant at that point, you will have to call it up by a separate procedure (described later).

- To create a *permanent* variant, precede its name with a slash mark (for example, */Short ME5A*). This variant will always appear hereafter whenever you call up this initial screen.

  For this example, we gave the variant the temporary name of *Short ME5A*.

Step 5. Enter a short description of the variant in the **Meaning field** (B).

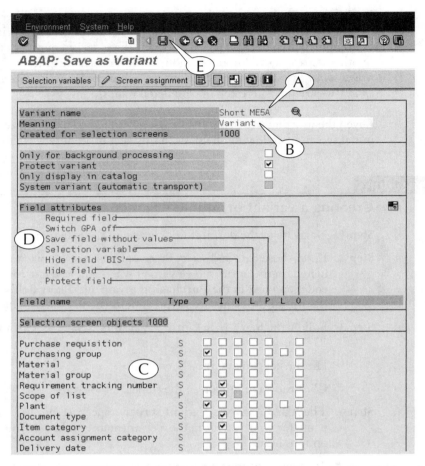

Figure 13.8   The **ABAP: Save as Variant screen** allows you to protect and hide selection criteria on an initial screen and create a screen variant. The top part only of this long screen is shown here.

Step 6.   Scroll down to the **Selection screen objects field area**. It contains a list of all the data entry fields and selection options on the initial screen (C). Each line is accompanied by several selection boxes. The key to these boxes appears in the **Field attributes field area** directly above them (D). The two critical selection boxes are *Protect field* and *Hide field*.

- Click the *Protect field selection box* for any data entry fields or selection options that you want to appear in an unalterable, prepopulated mode (with the entries and selections you made in Step 2) in the screen variant.

- Click the *Hide field selection box* for any data entry fields or selection options that you want to remove from the initial screen.

Step 7. Click the **Save button** (E) to save your input. The initial screen returns with a message in its status bar that the variant is saved Figure 13.9A).

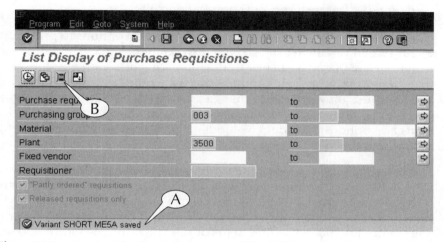

Figure 13.9 A variant for the initial screen of the *ME5A transaction*, trimmed in length and with our usual selection criteria protected.

End Procedure

Notice the convenient features of our screen variant.

- First, it is considerably shorter than the default screen because we hid the data entry fields and selection options that we never use. Every data entry field and selection option of importance appears "above the fold"—that is, we do not have to scroll down the length of the screen to find them.

- Second, the data entries and selections that we always make are prepopulated for us and grayed out so they cannot be changed (unless we decide to change the variant itself). We do not have to enter any codes—or even remember them, for that matter.

- Third, the screen still contains the other data entry fields that we use on occasion, so it is still very flexible in terms of its potential use.

A word of caution.

All in all, screen variants are tremendous time savers, particularly for transactions that you regularly set up and execute in the same manner. However, you should be careful about creating screen variants, and particularly creating permanent ones, because you can confuse yourself.

When we chose the data entry fields and selection options to protect and hide in our screen variant, we did so with the confidence that comes from ample experience with that particular transaction. We knew with absolute certainty that there were some fields and options that could be protected and prepopulated because they would not change as long as we still worked in the same office and did the same job. We also knew with equal certainty that there were fields and options that could be hidden because we would never use them, and other fields that had to remain available in case we wanted to use them.

The potential for confusion arises six months or a year after you create a screen variant, when you suddenly find yourself working in another department or with different job responsibilities. At that point, you might want to use this same transaction to generate a list of requisitions with different selection criteria, but you cannot find the data entry fields or selection options for these criteria on the initial screen—and you have forgotten that you are looking at a trimmed-down version of that initial screen, not the fuller default version.

So be careful with screen variants. Don't create a variant for the initial screen of a transaction until you are very familiar with that transaction and the many ways that you might use it at your job. And when you decide to create a variant, exercise some caution in the choices you make on the **ABAP: Save as Variant screen**, and leave some flexibility on the screen so that you can still use it for other purposes.

Changing a Screen Variant

When you navigate to the initial screen of a transaction and find a screen variant there, you can change it in one of two ways.

Procedure

Changing a Screen Variant

Step 1. Follow the menu path **Goto > Variant > Save as Variant** (Figure 13.7D).

Step 2. The **ABAP: Save as Variant screen** appears (Figure 13.8). Change the protect and hide selections for any data entry fields and selection options.

Step 3. *Option 1:* Save this revised version of the screen variant with the same name.

- Click the **Save button** (Figure 13.8E).

- The system responds with a popup screen that asks you to confirm the *overwrite* (or revision) of the variant (Figure 13.10).

- Hit the **Enter key** on your keyboard, *or*

 Click the **Yes button** on the popup screen (A).

 Option 2: Save this revision version of the screen variant as a new variant.

- Enter a name for the new variant in the **Variant name field** of the **ABAP: Save as Variant screen** (Figure 13.8A).

- Click the **Save button** (Figure 13.8E) to save the new variant and return to the initial screen, where it is now displayed.

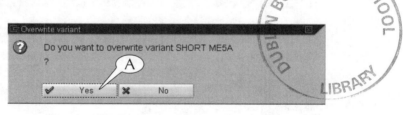

Figure 13.10   Confirm a change of a screen variant on the **Overwrite variant screen**.

End Procedure

Procedure

Restoring a Default Screen Variant

Step 1. Click the **All selections button** in the application toolbar of the screen variant (Figure 13.9B).

Step 2. The default version of the initial screen, with all its data entry fields and selection options, is displayed.

End Procedure

Calling Up a Screen Variant

If you create a *permanent* screen variant for a transaction (by attaching a slash to the beginning of its name), this customized version of the initial screen appears automatically when you navigate to it.

If you created a *temporary* screen variant for a transaction, the default version of the initial screen appears when you navigate to it. You can call up a screen variant by following this next procedure.

Procedure

Calling Up a Temporary Variant

Step 1. Once you arrive at the initial screen for the transaction, follow the menu path **Goto > Variants > Get** (Figure 13.11A).

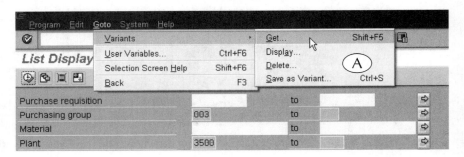

Figure 13.11   The menu path for calling up a temporary variant.

Step 2. The **Find Variant screen** appears (Figure 13.12) This is a search screen on which you can enter one or more search criteria. You have several options.

- Enter your name or SAP user ID in the **Created by field** (A), and the system searches for all the screen variants that you created for this transaction, *or*

  Enter part of the name of the variant, preceded and followed by asterisks (*), in the **Variant field** (B), *or*

  Do not make any entries, and the system searches for all the available screen variants for the initial screen.

  Once you complete this screen, click the **Execute button** (C).

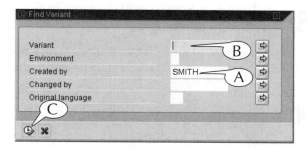

Figure 13.12   The **Find Variant screen** enables you to find a variant for an initial screen.

Step 3.   The **ABAP: Variant Directory of Program RM06BA00 screen** appears with a hit list of screen variants that match your search criteria (Figure 13.13). Locate the desired variant and double-click its name to call it up.

Note: You can arrange this list in the alphabetical or reverse-alphabetical order of either the **Variant name column** or the **Short description column** by clicking the header of one of those columns (A) and then clicking one of the two **Sort buttons** (B) in the upper-left corner of the screen.

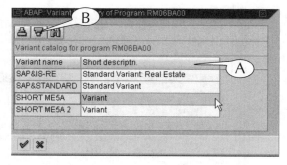

Figure 13.13   Display a screen variant on this popup screen by double-clicking it.

End Procedure

Deleting a Screen Variant

When you navigate to the initial screen of a transaction and find an unwanted screen variant there, you can delete it by following this next procedure.

Procedure

Deleting a Screen Variant

Step 1. Follow the menu path **Goto > Variants > Delete** (Figure 13.14A).

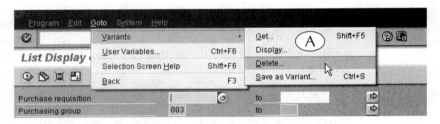

Figure 13.14   The menu path for deleting a screen variant.

Step 2. The **Find Variant screen** appears (Figure 13.15). This is a search screen on which you can enter one or more search criteria. Follow the instructions in Step 2 of the previous procedure (*Calling Up a Temporary Variant*) to use it.

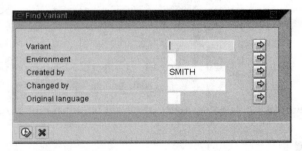

Figure 13.15   The **Find Variant screen** enables you to find a variant for an initial screen.

Step 3. The **Delete variants screen** appears (Figure 13.16). Double-click the name of the screen variant that you want to delete.

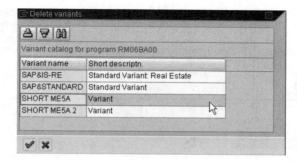

Figure 13.16   Select the screen variant to be deleted on this popup screen by double-clicking it.

Step 4. The **Delete variant screen** appears, asking you to confirm the deletion (Figure 13.17). Hit the **Enter key** on your keyboard.

Figure 13.17   Confirm the deletion of a variant on this screen.

Step 5. The **ABAP: Delete Variants screen** (Figure 13.18) appears, asking you to select one of two options: *In all clients* or *Only in current clients*. Select one, then click the **Continue button** (A).

Note: The usual choice is *In all clients*, but it can vary with the SAP system.

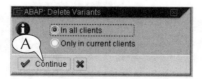

Figure 13.18   Delete the variant in all clients or just the one you're working in?

Step 6. The initial screen returns with a message in its status bar that the variant was deleted (Figure 13.19).

✅ Variant SHORT ME5A deleted

Figure 13.19 Confirmation that a screen variant is deleted is displayed in the status bar of the initial screen.

End Procedure

Single-Field Variants

You can quickly create a default data entry for any single field on an initial screen by following a simple shortcut procedure, rather than creating a full-blown screen variant. You have two options in this process.

- You can have the default data entry appear in a white, read/write field so that it can be changed if necessary.
- You can have the default data entry appear in a gray, read-only field so that it cannot be changed (that is, it is protected).

For an example, in this next procedure we create a default entry of *1000* for the **Plant field** of the initial screen in Figure 13.20.

Procedure

Creating a Single Default Data Entry on an Initial Screen

Step 1. Enter the default data in the field (A).

Step 2. Follow the menu path **System > User profile > Hold Data** to place the default data inside a white, read/write field, *or*

Follow the menu path **System > User profile > Set Data** to place the default data inside a gray, read-only field (B).

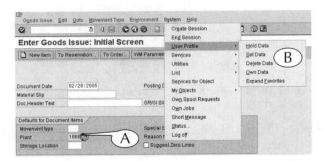

Figure 13.20 Creating a single default data entry via the **System > User profile menu**.

End Procedure

To undo this action:

Step 1. Click inside the field to select and highlight it.

Step 2. Follow the menu path **System** > **User profile** > **Delete Data**.

Part IV
WORKING WITH OUTPUT REPORTS

Just when I thought I was out, they pull me back in. — Michael Corleone (Al Pacino), Godfather III

Lesson 14

SORTING, FILTERING, AND SUMMING UP LINE-ITEM REPORTS

This is the first of two lessons on customizing the layouts and contents of line-item reports. It deals with the procedures for sorting, filtering, and summing up their data.

Line-item reports are the typical format for the output of *list-display transactions*, which generate lists of related objects (see the *Coda* at the end of this book) as well as the hit lists of code searches (see Lesson 10). They are also found on the initial and output screens of some *create*, *display*, and *change transactions*, including many purchasing and human resources transactions.

Each row in a line-item report displays the data about a single object, such as a vehicle, material, or business expenditure. The data are arrayed in columns, which are capped by **headers** that identify the data, and the rows are usually organized vertically by default according to the contents of the first column.

For example, we demonstrate some of the procedures in this lesson on the output of the *IH08 list-display transaction*. This output consists of a line-item report on mechanical equipment that is operated and maintained by physical plants in a company. When we run this transaction for plants in our company, the default output contains four columns of data (Figure 14.1):

- Equipment (that is, an equipment type code)
- Construction Year
- Description of technical object
- Acquisition value

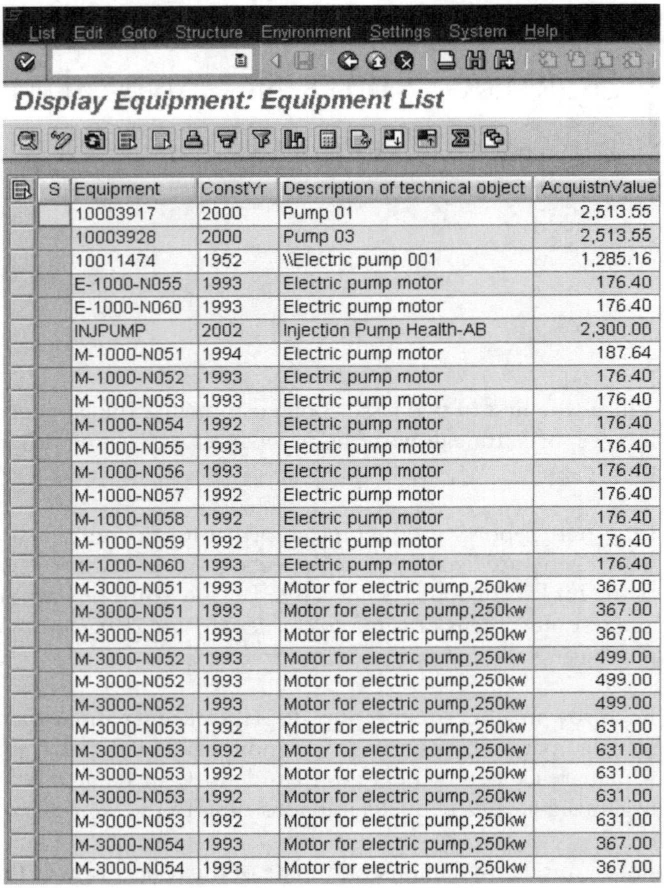

S	Equipment	ConstYr	Description of technical object	AcquistnValue
	10003917	2000	Pump 01	2,513.55
	10003928	2000	Pump 03	2,513.55
	10011474	1952	\\Electric pump 001	1,285.16
	E-1000-N055	1993	Electric pump motor	176.40
	E-1000-N060	1993	Electric pump motor	176.40
	INJPUMP	2002	Injection Pump Health-AB	2,300.00
	M-1000-N051	1994	Electric pump motor	187.64
	M-1000-N052	1993	Electric pump motor	176.40
	M-1000-N053	1993	Electric pump motor	176.40
	M-1000-N054	1992	Electric pump motor	176.40
	M-1000-N055	1993	Electric pump motor	176.40
	M-1000-N056	1993	Electric pump motor	176.40
	M-1000-N057	1992	Electric pump motor	176.40
	M-1000-N058	1992	Electric pump motor	176.40
	M-1000-N059	1992	Electric pump motor	176.40
	M-1000-N060	1993	Electric pump motor	176.40
	M-3000-N051	1993	Motor for electric pump,250kw	367.00
	M-3000-N051	1993	Motor for electric pump,250kw	367.00
	M-3000-N051	1993	Motor for electric pump,250kw	367.00
	M-3000-N052	1993	Motor for electric pump,250kw	499.00
	M-3000-N052	1993	Motor for electric pump,250kw	499.00
	M-3000-N052	1993	Motor for electric pump,250kw	499.00
	M-3000-N053	1992	Motor for electric pump,250kw	631.00
	M-3000-N053	1992	Motor for electric pump,250kw	631.00
	M-3000-N053	1992	Motor for electric pump,250kw	631.00
	M-3000-N053	1992	Motor for electric pump,250kw	631.00
	M-3000-N053	1992	Motor for electric pump,250kw	631.00
	M-3000-N054	1993	Motor for electric pump,250kw	367.00
	M-3000-N054	1993	Motor for electric pump,250kw	367.00

Figure 14.1 The default version of the output of the *IH08 transaction* is a line-item report with four columns of data. Each line displays the data on one piece of equipment.

However, you can change the default layout and content of a line-item report directly on its output screen in several ways. For example, we customized our sample report in these ways, which are shown in Figure 14.2.

- We arranged or *sorted* the line items in order of their equipment code, then clustered those line items with the same code so that they appear as **groups** in the first column.
- Within each group, we sorted the line items in order of their construction year, then clustered those line items with the same construction year so that they appear as **subgroups** in the second column.

- We filtered the report to eliminate line items with an acquisition value of less than $1,000. (Notice the absence of any dollar value less than $1,000 in the **Acquisition value column**.)

- We attached a grand total for the acquisition values of all the equipment to the very bottom line of the report (A).

- We subtotaled the acquisition values for each equipment-code group (for example, B) and construction-year subgroup (for example, C).

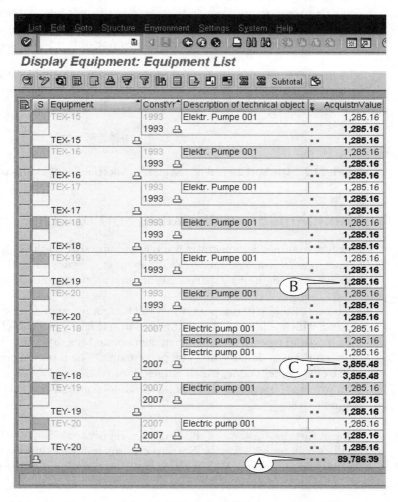

Figure 14.2 Our version of the output of the *IH08 transaction*, after we customized the line-item report with filters, sorts, and sums.

We demonstrate in this lesson the procedures for customizing line-item reports in these ways, using examples from several initial screens, output screens and the hit lists of search screens.

Sorting and Grouping Line-item Reports

The **sorting** function rearranges the rows of line-item reports according to the contents of one or more selected data columns (which we call the *sorting columns*). You can rearrange these rows in either alphanumerical (for example, *A to Z* or *1 to 1000*) or reverse alphanumerical order in one of two ways.

The first method makes use of the **Sort ascending** (A) and **Sort descending** (B) **buttons** (Figure 14.3). We demonstrate their use in the next three examples.

Figure 14.3   The **Sort ascending** (A) and **Sort descending** (B) **buttons**.

Example 1: Single-Column Sort of a Line-item Report

Our first example demonstrates a single-column sort on the output of the *Cost Center Actual/Plan/Variance (A/P/V) transaction*[1] (Figure 14.4). This transaction displays the budget of a department (or *cost center*) in a line-item format.

Each row of the A/P/V report shows the budget for a single cost category or *cost element*, which is identified in its first column (Figure 14.4). Each row displays the *actual* and *planned costs* for a cost element and the difference or *variance* between them in dollar values and percentages. The report is organized in order of the cost element code, which ranges from *400000* to *799000*. This sorting column (the first) is automatically highlighted to distinguish it from the other data columns.

We can sort the contents of this line-item report according to the contents of another column by using the **Sort ascending** and **Sort descending buttons** in its application toolbar (A). For an example, we can rearrange the rows in order of

---

1. We have not used the transaction code in this name because it is very long and clumsy: *S_ALR_87013611*.

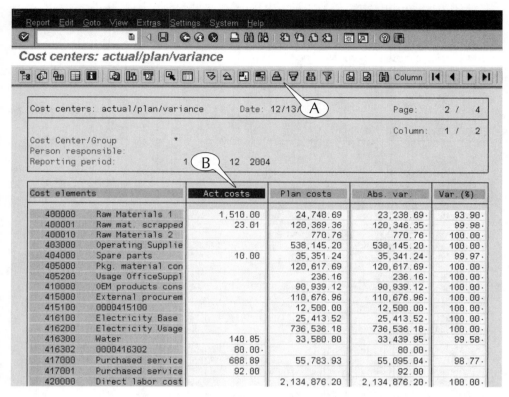

Figure 14.4 The default output of the *Cost Center Actual/Plan/Variance transaction*, with the rows sorted in order of increasing cost element code.

their actual costs, with those rows with the highest costs at the top of the report and those with the lowest at the bottom, by following this two-step procedure.

Procedure

Single-Column Sort of a Line-item Report

Step 1. Click the header of the **Actual costs column** (Figure 14.4B) to select and highlight it.

Step 2. Click the **Sort descending button**.

This procedure reorganized the report so that its rows are organized in order of descending actual costs (Figure 14.5). In addition, it placed a **sort-descending icon** in the header of the **Actual Costs column** (A) to indicate that the report is arranged in that order.

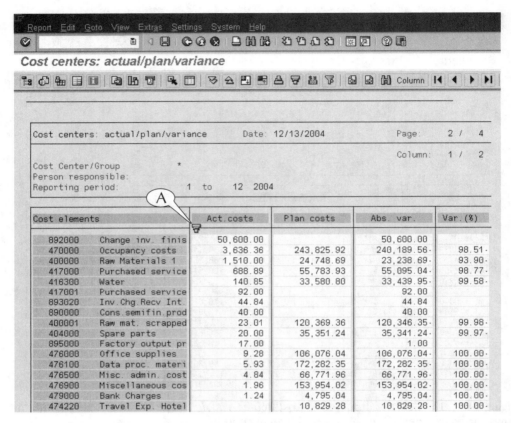

Figure 14.5   The customized output of the *Cost Center Actual/Plan/Variance transaction*, with the rows sorted in order of descending actual costs.

End Procedure

Example 2: Multiple-Column Sort of a Line-item Report

This second example demonstrates a multiple-column sort on the output of the *IH08 transaction*, which displays data about equipment in a line-item format. The rows in the default version of this report are organized in order of the equipment code, which appears in the first column (Figure 14.6).

We can rearrange this report so that the rows are organized first in order of increasing equipment code (we will call this the "primary sorting column"), then in order of increasing construction year (we will call this the "secondary sorting column"), by following this next procedure.

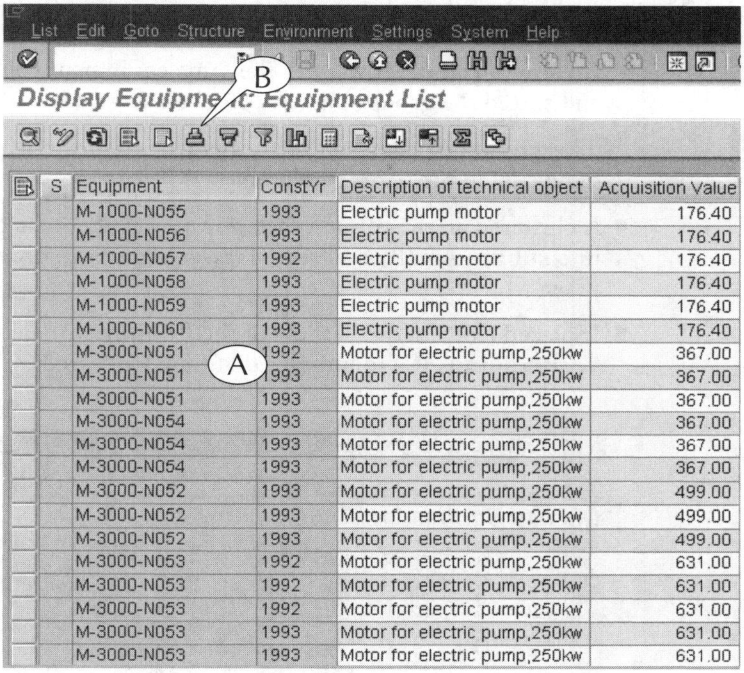

Figure 14.6   The default output of the *IH08 transaction,* with the rows sorted in order of increasing equipment code.

<hr>

Procedure

Multiple-Column Sort of a Line-item Report

Step 1. Click-and-drag across the headers of the sorting columns (if they are next to one another) to select and highlight them (A).

Note: When you use this method, the first (left) column becomes the primary sorting column, the second becomes the secondary sorting column, and so on. See the next lesson for instructions on rearranging the orders of columns if it is necessary.

or alternatively

Press and hold the **Ctrl key** on your keyboard, click the headers of the sorting columns to select and highlight them, then release the **Ctrl key**.

Note: When you use this method, click the primary sorting column first, the secondary sorting column second, and so on.

Step 2. Click the **Sort ascending button** (B) in the application toolbar.

This procedure had *three* effects on the line-item report (Figure 14.7):

- It clustered all the rows with the same equipment code into **groups** (A), and sorted the groups in order of increasing code.

  This grouping occurs automatically whenever there are rows with the same data in the sorting columns.

- It clustered all the rows in each group with the same construction year into **subgroups** (B), and sorted the subgroups in order of increasing year.

- It placed icons in the headers of the **Equipment** and **Construction Year columns** (C) to indicate that they are sorted.

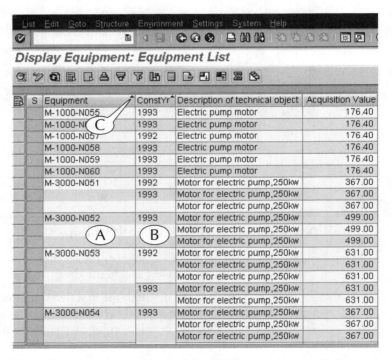

Figure 14.7   The customized output of the *IH08 transaction*, with the rows grouped and sorted by model number and construction year.

End Procedure

Example 3: Single-Column Sort of a Hit List

This third example demonstrates the method of sorting the hit lists of search screens.

Search hit lists are usually displayed in a line-item format, and occasionally you will see the **Sort ascending** and **Sort descending buttons** somewhere on their screens (see Figure 13.13 on page 163 for an example). When this occurs, you can use the same procedures that were described in the last two examples to rearrange their contents.

When the hit list screen does not display these two buttons, you can still rearrange their contents by simply double-clicking the header of a data column.

For example, the hit list for a search for plant codes is a two-column line-item report (Figure 14.8A). However, it is organized in order of the plant code, and the plant names are randomly organized. When you scroll through the hit list, it is hard to find a plant by its name because of this lack of organization.

You can solve this problem by double-clicking the header of the **Name column**: One double-click reorganizes it in alphabetical order (B), and a second click reorganizes it in reverse alphabetical order (not shown here).

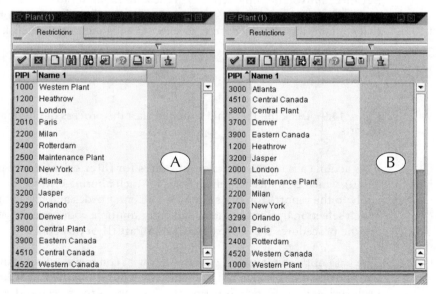

Figure 14.8 The hit list for a plant code search, in the default order (A) and reorganized in order of plant name (B).

We described the means of reorganizing the line-item reports of output screens and hit lists here. You will also find line-item tables on the screens of some *create*, *display*, and *change transactions*. They can be reorganized in the same manner.

For instance, the initial screen of the *ME51N transaction*, which creates requisitions for materials and services, contains a line-item table for entering data about those items (see Figure 9.3 on page 106). This table has its own application toolbar, which includes the **Sort ascending** and **Sort descending buttons**. You can use them in the same way that you would use them on an output screen.

Filtering Line-item Reports

The **filtering** function edits the contents of line-item reports and shortens them by removing rows that contain certain data values, or *filtering criteria*, in specified columns.

You can filter a report whenever you see the **Threshold button** (also called the **Set filter button** on some screens) in the application toolbar of the output screen of a report (Figure 14.9). To start this procedure, click the header of the column that contains the filtering criteria to select and highlight it, then click this button.

Figure 14.9 Click the **Threshold button** to start the process of filtering line-item reports.

This action calls up the **Determine values for filter criteria screen** (Figure 14.10), which contains data entry fields for each filtering criteria that you want to apply to the report. You can search for and enter codes and texts in these fields, attach selection options to them, and enter multiple codes and ranges, by following the procedures that were described in Part III of this book.

The base of the filter screen contains a row of command buttons, including the **Enter button** (A), which has the same effect as hitting the **Enter key** on your keyboard, and the **Cancel button** (B), which erases the screen and returns you to the main screen. You can delete one filtering criterion by clicking inside one of its data entry fields and then clicking the **Delete row button** (C), or you can delete all the filtering criteria on the screen by simply clicking the **Delete button** (D).

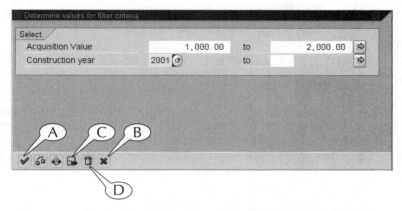

Figure 14.10   Enter your filter criteria on the **Determine values for filter criteria screen** as you would enter them on any initial screen.

*Don't see the **Threshold button** on your screen?* Follow the menu path **Settings > Options** to call up the **Options screen** (Figure 14.11), select the *Expert mode option* (A) and hit the **Enter key** on your keyboard.

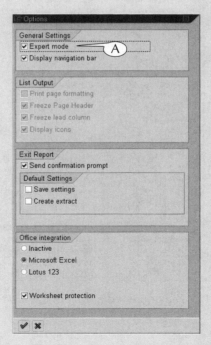

Figure 14.11   You must select the *Expert mode option* on the **Options screen** in order to see the **Threshold button** on the output screen.

We now illustrate the filtering of line-item reports with two examples.

Example 1: Filtering the Line-item Report of the IH08 Transaction

Once again, we use the output of the *IH08 transaction*, which displays data about equipment, to demonstrate the procedure for filtering a line-item report. The report is generated by a list-display transaction, and it was originally set up to display data on *every* pump operated and maintained by a physical plant (Figure 14.12).

Display Equipment: Equipment List

S	Equipment	Description of technical object	Acquisition Value	ConstYr
	10003917	Pump 01	2,513.55	2000
	10003928	Pump 03	2,513.55	2000
	10011474	\\Electric pump 001	1,285.16	1952
	E-1000-N055	Electric pump motor	176.40	1993
	E-1000-N060	Electric pump motor	176.40	1993
	INJPUMP	Injection Pump Health-AB	2,300.00	2002
	M-1000-N051	Electric pump motor	187.64	1994
	M-1000-N052	Electric pump motor	176.40	1993
	M-1000-N053	Electric pump motor	176.40	1993
	M-1000-N054	Electric pump motor	176.40	1992
	M-1000-N055	Electric pump motor	176.40	1993
	M-1000-N056	Electric pump motor	176.40	1993
	M-1000-N057	Electric pump motor	176.40	1992
	M-1000-N058	Electric pump motor	176.40	1992
	M-1000-N059	Electric pump motor	176.40	1992
	M-1000-N060	Electric pump motor	176.40	1993
	M-3000-N051	Motor for electric pump,250kw	367.00	1993
	M-3000-N051	Motor for electric pump,250kw	367.00	1993
	M-3000-N051	Motor for electric pump,250kw	367.00	1993
	M-3000-N052	Motor for electric pump,250kw	499.00	1993
	M-3000-N052	Motor for electric pump,250kw	499.00	1993
	M-3000-N052	Motor for electric pump,250kw	499.00	1993
	M-3000-N053	Motor for electric pump,250kw	631.00	1992
	M-3000-N053	Motor for electric pump,250kw	631.00	1992
	M-3000-N053	Motor for electric pump,250kw	631.00	1992
	M-3000-N053	Motor for electric pump,250kw	631.00	1992
	M-3000-N053	Motor for electric pump,250kw	631.00	1992
	M-3000-N054	Motor for electric pump,250kw	367.00	1993
	M-3000-N054	Motor for electric pump,250kw	367.00	1993
	M-3000-N054	Motor for electric pump,250kw	367.00	1993

Figure 14.12 The unfiltered output of the *IH08 transaction*.

Suppose we want to limit this line-item report to all those pumps in our plant that cost between $1,000 and $2,000. We can edit it along those lines by following this next procedure.

Filtering a Line-item Report

Step 1. Click the header of the **Acquisition value column** (A) to select and highlight it, then click the **Threshold button** (B).

Step 2. The **Determine values for filter criteria screen** appears with data entry fields for the acquisition value (Figure 14.13).

- Enter *1000* in the first field and *2000* in the second field. Do not use commas or dollar signs.

- Hit the **Enter key** on your keyboard.

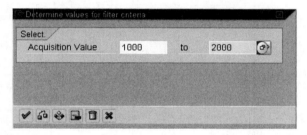

Figure 14.13 Filtering the report to limit it to pumps with acquisition values of $1,000 to $2,000.

Step 3. The line-item report returns, and now displays only the data for pumps with an acquisition value of $1,000 to $2,000 (Figure 14.14). A small icon also appears in the header of the **Acquisition value column** (A) to indicate that the report is filtered according to the contents of that column.

Suppose we want to further limit this report to all pumps that were constructed after 2001. We would continue in this way:

Step 4. Click the header of the **Construction year column** (Figure 14.14B) to select and highlight it, then click the **Threshold button** (C).

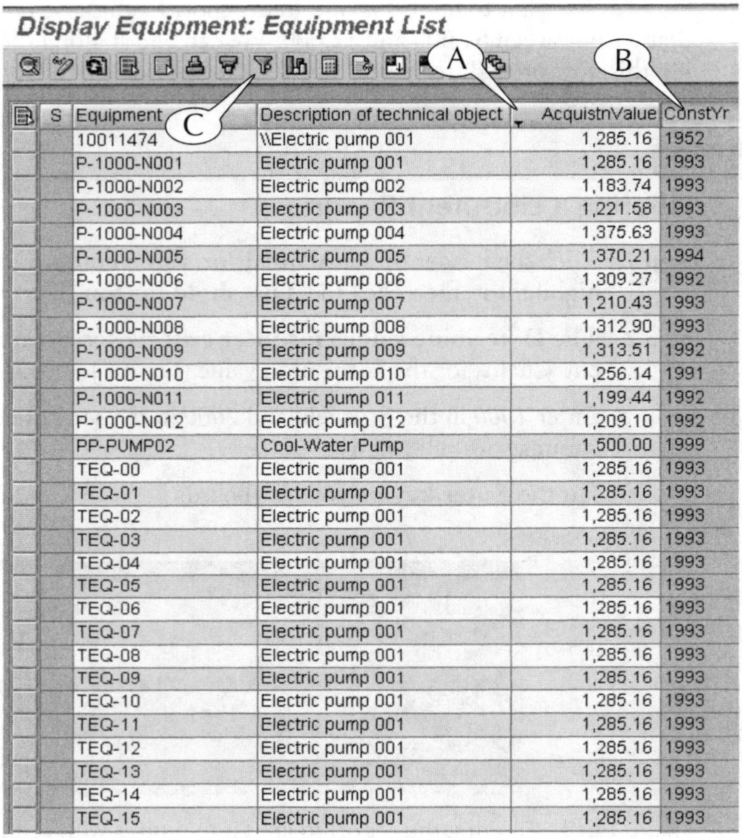

Figure 14.14   The filtered output of the *IH08 transaction*.

Step 5. The **Determine values for filter criteria screen** returns with a second set of data entry fields for the construction year (Figure 14.15A).

- Double-click inside the first of the two **Construction year fields** to call up the **Maintain Selection Option screen** (see Figure 12.3 on page 144), and double-click the *green greater than (>) option* to attach it to the **Construction year fields** (B).

- Enter *2001* in the first **Construction year field**.

- Hit the **Enter key** on your keyboard.

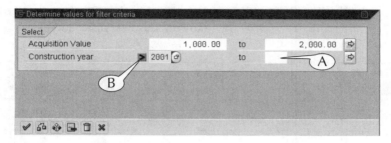

Figure 14.15   Adding a second filter to the output of the *IH08 transaction*, this time using a selection option.

Step 6.   The line-item report returns, and now displays only the data for those pumps that were acquired after 2001 at a cost of $1,000 to $2,000 (Figure 14.16).

Display Equipment: Equipment List

	S	Equipment	Description of technical object	AcquistnValue	ConstYr
		TEY-18	Electric pump 001	1,285.16	2007
		TEY-18	Electric pump 001	1,285.16	2007
		TEY-18	Electric pump 001	1,285.16	2007
		TEY-19	Electric pump 001	1,285.16	2007
		TEY-20	Electric pump 001	1,285.16	2007

Figure 14.16   The twice-filtered output of the *IH08 transaction*.

End Procedure

Example 2: Filtering the Line-item Report of the Cost Center A/P/V Transaction

We return to the output of the *Cost Center Actual/Plan/Variance (A/P/V) transaction* (Figure 14.17) to demonstrate the use of a second filtering screen that you may encounter in some modules.

We filter this line-item report according to the contents of the **Abs variance column** (A), which shows the numerical differences between the actual and planned costs of cost elements. Notice that some of the values in this column are positive, and some are negative. We can apply a filter to the report that removes those line items with variance values less than $5,000, *regardless of whether they are positive or negative*, by following this next procedure.

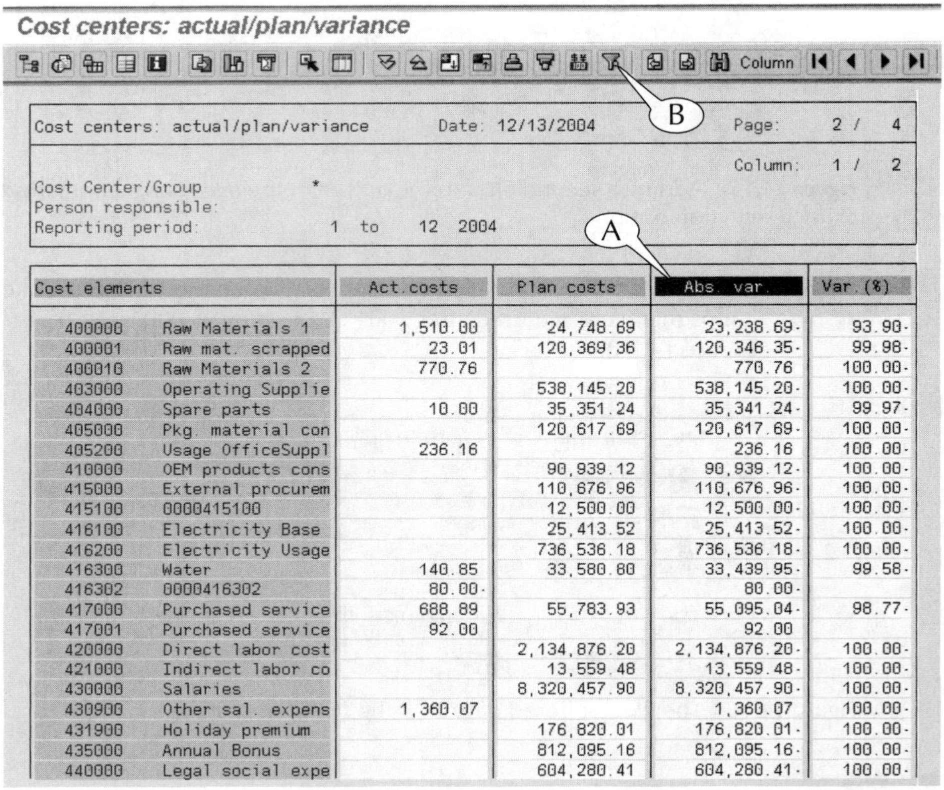

Cost centers: actual/plan/variance

Figure 14.17   The default output of the *Cost Center Actual/Plan/Variance transaction*. Notice that there are positive and negative dollar values in the **Abs var column**.

Procedure

Filtering Positive and Negative Values in a Line-item Report 1

Step 1.   Click the header of the **Abs var column** to select and highlight it (Figure 14.17A), then click the **Threshold button** (B).

Step 2.   The **Maintain Threshold Value Conditions for Selection 001 screen** appears (Figure 14.18). It contains two sets of identical field areas in which you can apply one or two filters. We use the first set of field areas in the top half of the screen to apply one filter in this procedure.

- Select the *Active option* (A) to activate the top filter.

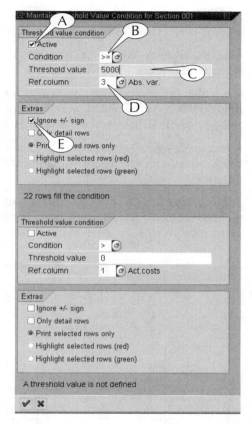

Figure 14.18 The **Maintain Threshold Value Conditions screen** contains field areas for two separate filters. We use it to apply one filter to the report.

Step 3. Enter the *greater than or equal to* (>=) *condition code* in the **Condition field** (B) by doing the following.

- Click inside the field to call up the **Threshold value condition search screen** (Figure 14.19).

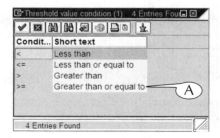

Figure 14.19 Select a condition code from this screen.

- ▪ Double-click the *greater than or equal to condition code* (A), and it is entered in the **Condition field** (Figure 14.18B).

Step 4. Enter *5000* (again, without a dollar sign or comma) in the **Threshold value field** (Figure 14.18C).

Step 5. Verify that the correct filtering column is entered in the **Ref column field** (D). If it is not, click its search button to call up a list of columns, and double-click the correct one to enter it there.

Step 6. Select the *Ignore +/- sign option* (E). This action sets the filter to remove all line items with variances less than $5,000 whether they are positive or negative.

Step 7. Hit the **Enter key** on your keyboard to return to the output screen, where the filter is now applied to the line-item report (Figure 14.20). Notice that a filter icon (A) is attached to the header of the **Abs var column**.

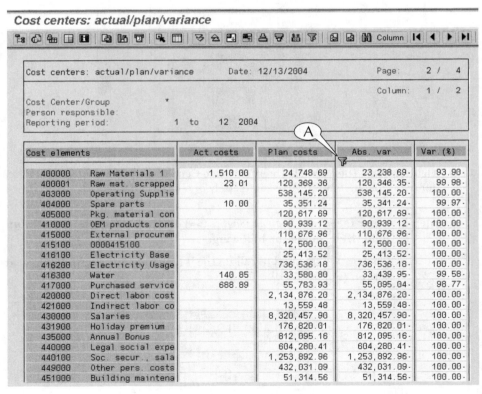

Figure 14.20   The filtered output of the *Cost Center Actual/Plan/Variance transaction*, with all line items with variances less than $5,000 removed.

End Procedure

Once you apply a filter by this procedure, you can remove it by recalling the **Maintain Threshold Value Conditions screen** and deselecting the *Active option* (Figure 14.18A).

Example 3: Filtering Positive and Negative Values on the Usual Filter Screen

The **Maintain Threshold Value Conditions for Selection 001 screen** (Figure 14.18) is associated with only a few output screens in SAP. However, it is quite convenient for filtering numerical data with both positive and negative values, thanks to the *Ignore +/- option*.

You may encounter positive and negative numerical values on other line-item reports where you have the usual **Determine values for filter criteria screen** at your disposal for filtering them. In these cases, filtering positive and negative numerical values is a little more cumbersome.

For example, consider the example of the line-item report on the **Display Actual Cost Line Items for Orders screen** (Figure 14.21). This report contains the **Val in rep cur column** (A), which displays both positive (credit) and negative (debit) dollar values. If you want to filter this report according to the contents of this column, you will find that the **Determine values for filter criteria screen** contains data entry fields for these dollar values, but no handy *Ignore +/- option* (Figure 14.22).

Figure 14.21   The line-item report of the **Display Actual Cost Line Items for Order screen** contains the **Val in rep cur column,** where you will find positive and negative dollar values.

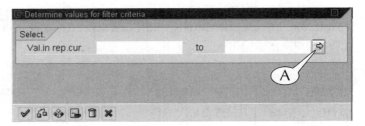

Figure 14.22   Use the multiple selection screen of the **Val in rep cur fields** to filter a data column of positive and negative values.

To apply a filter to these dollar values that takes into account their positive and negative values, you must use the multiple selection option on the **Determine values for filter criteria screen**.

For example, if we wanted to apply the same filter that we used in the previous example, we could click the multiple selection button for the **Val in rep cur fields** on the filter screen (Figure 14.22A) to call up a multiple selection screen (Figure 14.23), and then do the following.

- Click the green **Single vals tab** (Figure 14.23A).

- Enter *5000* in the first field of that screen, and attach a *greater than or equal to selection option* to it. This action filters out all positive values less than $5,000.

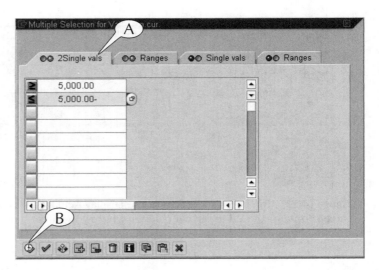

Figure 14.23   Setting up the multiple selection screen to filter out dollar values less than $5,000, whether they are positive or negative.

- Enter -*5000* in the second field of that screen, and attach a *less than or equal to selection option* to it. This action filters out all negative values greater than $5,000 (that is, between 0 and -5000).

- Hit the **Copy button** (B) to save your entries and return to the **Determine values for filter criteria screen**.

- Hit the **Enter key** on your keyboard to save your filter and return to the output screen, where the data would be filtered.

We could also set up the multiple selection screen in this way (Figure 14.24):

- Click the red **Interval tab** (A).

- Enter -*5000* and *5000* in the first line of paired fields. This action filters out all values within this range.

- Hit the **Copy button** (B) to save your entries and return to the **Determine values for filter criteria screen**.

- Hit the **Enter key** on your keyboard to save your filter and return to the output screen, where the data would be filtered.

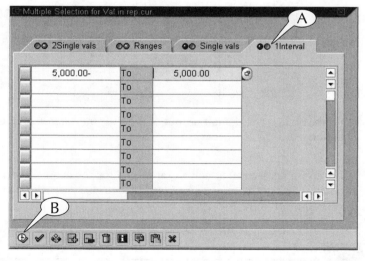

Figure 14.24   Setting up the multiple selection screen to filter out dollar values between -$5,000 and $5,000.

Summing Up Data Columns in Line-item Reports

You can attach grand totals beneath the bottom lines of data columns, as well as subtotals beneath the bottom lines of groups and subgroups, in line-item reports. This is possible whenever you see the **Summation button** in the application toolbar of the output screen for the report (Figure 14.25A). This button can only be applied to columns with data such as dollar values and total quantities. It cannot be applied to columns with dates, model number, object codes, text, and the like.

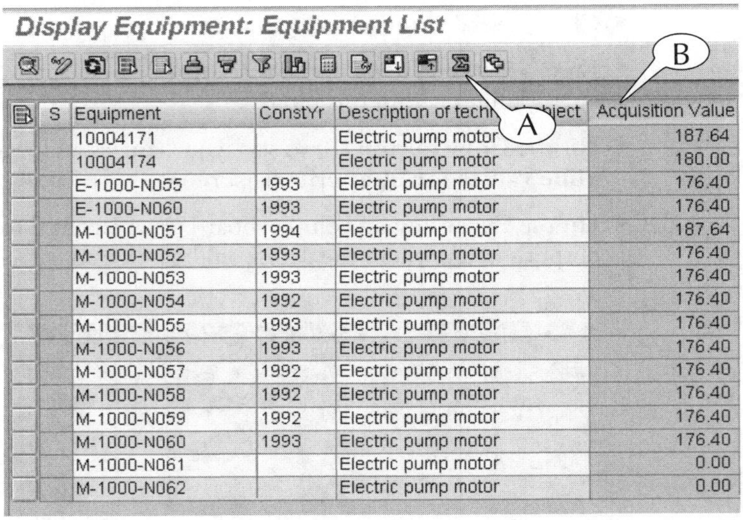

Display Equipment: Equipment List

S	Equipment	ConstYr	Description of tech object	Acquisition Value
	10004171		Electric pump motor	187.64
	10004174		Electric pump motor	180.00
	E-1000-N055	1993	Electric pump motor	176.40
	E-1000-N060	1993	Electric pump motor	176.40
	M-1000-N051	1994	Electric pump motor	187.64
	M-1000-N052	1993	Electric pump motor	176.40
	M-1000-N053	1993	Electric pump motor	176.40
	M-1000-N054	1992	Electric pump motor	176.40
	M-1000-N055	1993	Electric pump motor	176.40
	M-1000-N056	1993	Electric pump motor	176.40
	M-1000-N057	1992	Electric pump motor	176.40
	M-1000-N058	1992	Electric pump motor	176.40
	M-1000-N059	1992	Electric pump motor	176.40
	M-1000-N060	1993	Electric pump motor	176.40
	M-1000-N061		Electric pump motor	0.00
	M-1000-N062		Electric pump motor	0.00

Figure 14.25   The default output of the *IH08 transaction* and its **Summation button** (A).

For example, we can attach a grand total for the acquisition value beneath the bottom line of the line-item report of the *IH08 transaction* with this two-step procedure (Figure 14.25).

Procedure

Summing Up Data in a Column of a Line-item Report

Step 1. Click the header of the **Acquisition value column** to select and high-light it (B).

Step 2. Click the **Summation button** (A), and the grand total for the selected column appears in a highlighted line at the very bottom of the screen (Figure 14.26A).

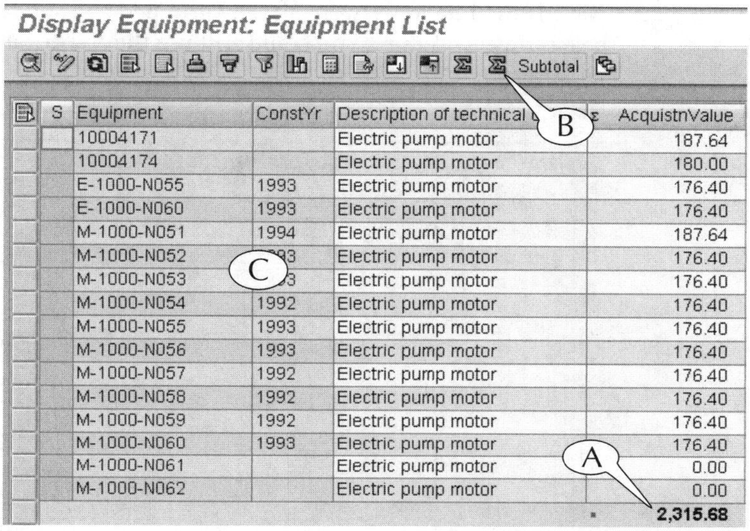

Figure 14.26   A grand total appears for the **Acquisition value column** at the bottom of the line-item report.

End Procedure

As soon as we added a grand total to this report, the **Subtotal button** (Figure 14.26B) appears in the application toolbar of its screen. We can use this button to simultaneously group and subtotal line items in this same report.

For an example, we group and subgroup the line items in our sample report by equipment code and construction year, respectively, and subtotal their acquisition values by following this next procedure.

Procedure

Grouping and Subtotaling Data in a Line-item Report

Step 1.   Click-and-drag across the headers of the **Equipment code** and **Construction year columns** to select and highlight them (C), *or*

Press and hold the **Ctrl key** on your keyboard, click the headers of the two columns to select and highlight them, then release the **Ctrl key**.

Step 2.   Click the **Subtotal button** (B). The line items are automatically grouped and subgrouped, and subtotals for the acquisition value appear on the bottom line of each group and subgroup (Figure 14.27).

Note: If the line items were already grouped and subgrouped before you began this procedure, you could still use the **Subtotal button** for this same result.

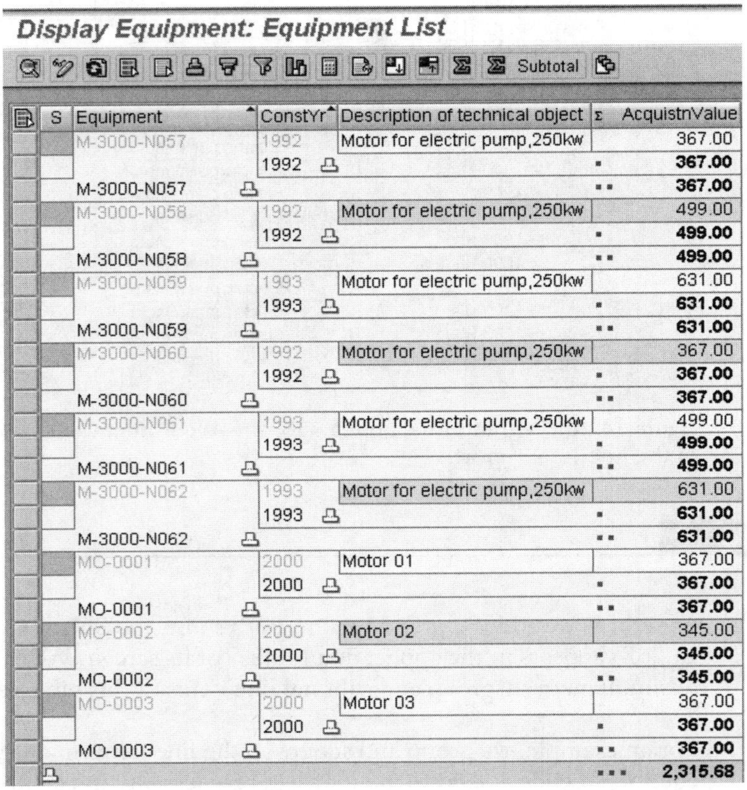

Display Equipment: Equipment List

S	Equipment	ConstYr	Description of technical object	Σ	AcquisitnValue
	M-3000-N057	1992	Motor for electric pump,250kw		367.00
		1992		▪	**367.00**
	M-3000-N057			▪▪	**367.00**
	M-3000-N058	1992	Motor for electric pump,250kw		499.00
		1992		▪	**499.00**
	M-3000-N058			▪▪	**499.00**
	M-3000-N059	1993	Motor for electric pump,250kw		631.00
		1993		▪	**631.00**
	M-3000-N059			▪▪	**631.00**
	M-3000-N060	1992	Motor for electric pump,250kw		367.00
		1992		▪	**367.00**
	M-3000-N060			▪▪	**367.00**
	M-3000-N061	1993	Motor for electric pump,250kw		499.00
		1993		▪	**499.00**
	M-3000-N061			▪▪	**499.00**
	M-3000-N062	1993	Motor for electric pump,250kw		631.00
		1993		▪	**631.00**
	M-3000-N062			▪▪	**631.00**
	MO-0001	2000	Motor 01		367.00
		2000		▪	**367.00**
	MO-0001			▪▪	**367.00**
	MO-0002	2000	Motor 02		345.00
		2000		▪	**345.00**
	MO-0002			▪▪	**345.00**
	MO-0003	2000	Motor 03		367.00
		2000		▪	**367.00**
	MO-0003			▪▪	**367.00**
				▪▪▪	**2,315.68**

Figure 14.27 Groups and subgroups of line items, each with their own bottom-line subtotal of acquisition values.

End Procedure

Lesson 15
DISPLAY VARIANTS FOR LINE-ITEM REPORTS

This is the second of two lessons on customizing the layouts and contents of line-item reports. It deals with the procedures for creating and working with **display variants**.

Line-item reports are the typical format for the output of *list-display transactions*, which generate lists of related objects (see the *Coda* at the end of this book) as well as the hit lists of code searches (see Lesson 10). They are also found on the initial and output screens of some *create*, *display*, and *change transactions*, including many purchasing and human resources transactions.

Each row in a line-item report displays the data about a single object, such as a vehicle, material, or business expenditure. The data are arrayed in columns, which are capped by **headers** that identify the data, and the rows are usually organized vertically by default according to the contents of the first column. However, the content and layout of a line-item report—the data it displays and the ways in which the data are arranged vertically and horizontally—are usually fixed by computer programmers, with the help of functional experts, when SAP is configured for your company. They may not necessarily meet *your* needs or interests as a user of the system.

For example, we demonstrate the procedures for creating and working with display variants in this lesson with the output of the *KSB1 transaction*. This output consists of a line-item report of the *actual costs* or expenditures for a department (or *cost center*) in a business or an organization. We run this transaction periodically for our department to keep track of our costs and to monitor the status of our budget. The output of this transaction displays these data about our costs on each line of the report by default (Figure 15.1):

- The number and name of the *cost element* or cost category (such as salary, travel, and lodging) in the first two columns

- The dollar value of the cost in the **Val in rep curr column**

- The currency type in the **Obj curr column**

- The total quantity

- The name and number of the *offsetting account* (the corporate ledger account from which costs are ultimately paid, which is not the same as our department budget account) in the last two columns

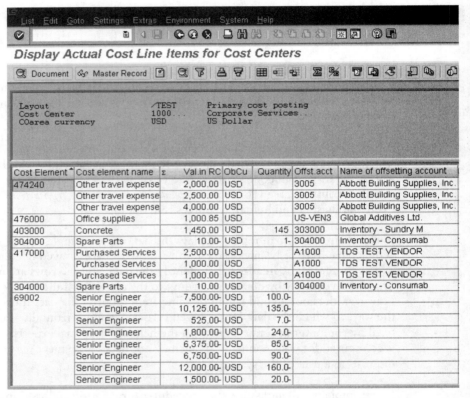

Figure 15.1   The default version of the output report of the *KSB1 transaction*.

This is not an especially useful report for us, for several reasons.

- It displays both the name *and* the number of the cost element in two columns. This is redundant. We need only one of these two bits of data—preferably, the name of the cost element.

- It displays the currency type. While our company is global in reach, all our costs are incurred in the United States, where the currency is always U.S. dollars, and so this column of data is not necessary.

- It contains a column for the total quantity, which is meaningless when dealing with salaries and other types of costs—so much so, in fact, that there are usually no data in this column.

- It displays both the name *and* number of the offsetting account in two columns. Once again, this is redundant, but more important, these are the sorts of data that our accountant needs to worry about, not us.

- It does not display data on who spent our money, what exactly they spent it on, and what document they filed in the database to charge the cost to our account (very useful in case we need to have our accountant verify a charge).

To satisfy our business needs, we created a display variant for the output of the *KSB1 transaction* (Figure 15.2). This customized version of the line-item report displays these data for each cost:

- The cost element name (but not the number)

- The name, business group code (**User**), and department code (**PaCC**) of the person who charged the cost to our account

- The dollar amount of the charge (**Val in RC**—representative currency)

- The number of the fiscal document that was created in SAP to charge that cost to our account

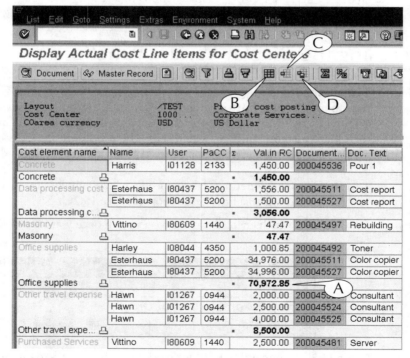

Figure 15.2   Our display variant for the output report of the *KSB1 transaction*.

- The document header text, which is a brief description of the nature of the expenditure that was charged to our account

In addition, we modified the layout of this line-item report to do the following:

- Display a grand total of all our expenditures at the bottom of the **Val in RC column**

- Group the line items by the cost element name, and subtotal the costs for all the line items in each cost-element group (A)

This customized report is far more useful for our purposes, because it tells us in a nutshell who (by name and affiliation) spent our hard-earned money on what (by cost element name and document header text). In addition, it provides a document number that we can pass to our accountant in case we have questions about a charge to our account. Finally, it contains no data about offsetting accounts, currency type, or anything else that is either obvious or not of interest to us, so it is brief and to the point.

Line-item reports are one of the most common transactions that are executed in SAP, and display variants are a powerful tool for customizing their contents and layouts. This lesson provides instructions on creating and using display variants.

Accessing the Display Variant Functions

You can create a display variant for a line-item report whenever you see either the **Change layout button** (Figure 15.2B) or **Current display variant button** (Figure 15.3A) in the application toolbar of its output screen. Wherever you see the **Change layout button**, which starts the procedure for creating a display variant, it is accompanied by two other buttons for working with display variants:

- **Choose** (sometimes labeled **Get**), which enables you to apply an existing variant to a line-item report (Figure 15.2C)

- **Save**, which enables you to save a variant once you create it (Figure 15.2D)

Figure 15.3 Command buttons for working with display variants are found in the application toolbars of many output screens.

(The **Change Layout button** is not usually accompanied by these two buttons, however.)

In addition to these buttons, you can also follow the menu path **Settings > Layout** to display four commands for working with display variants (Figure 15.4). Three of these commands are redundant with the buttons in the application toolbar.

- *Change* (or *Current* on some screens), which begins the procedure for creating a display variant

- *Choose* (or *Get* on some screens), which enables you to apply an existing display variant to a line-item report

- *Save*, which enables you to save a display variant once you create it

- *Administration* (or *Manage* or *Management* on some screens), which enables you to delete an existing variant (and the only variant command without a corresponding button in the application toolbar)

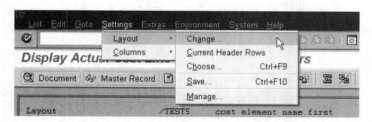

Figure 15.4   The menu bar of all output screens contains all four commands for working with display variants. The menu path for starting the procedure for creating a display variant is shown here.

You may be asking yourself, *Why are there two separate sets of buttons and commands for executing the same functions in a software application?*

The reason for this discrepancy is that SAP is not really a single software application, but a set of separately developed applications that are programmed to work together. Consequently, design changes that are made in some modules are not always immediately carried over into other modules.

Where such discrepancies occur, we identify all the alternative buttons and commands that you might encounter throughout SAP.

The Change Layout Screen

The first few steps in the procedure for creating a display variant are carried out on the **Change Layout screen** (Figure 15.5). You can call up this screen in one of two ways.

- Click the **Change layout** or **Current display variant button** in the application toolbar (Figures 15.2B and 15.3A), *or*

  Follow the menu path **Setting > Layout > Change** *or* **Current** (Figure 15.4).

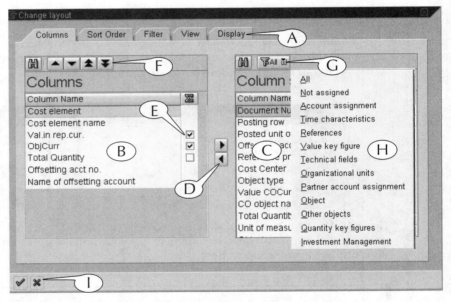

Figure 15.5   The menu path for starting the procedure for creating a display variant.

The **Change Layout screen** contains a row of five tabs at the top (A). The first tab is selected by default to display the **Column subscreen**, which is the main working environment on the screen.

The **Column subscreen** is dominated by the **Columns** (B) and **Column Set** (C) **windows**. They are separated by two **control arrows**, which you use for transferring datatypes between them (D).

The **Columns window** displays a list of all the datatypes that appear in the *original* version of the line-item report. This list is often accompanied by the

selection boxes of the **Summation column** (E), which you can click to attach totals to the bottoms of numerical data columns. The **Columns window** is overlain by the **Search button** (which we never use) and four **positioning buttons** (F), which you use to change the horizontal order of the data columns in the display variant.

The **Column Set window** displays the names of other datatypes that are available for the report. It is overlain by the **Search button** (again, which we never use) and the **Filter button** (G), which controls the display inside the window. When this latter button reads *All* (its default setting), the display shows *all* the available datatypes for the report. However, you can limit the display to a particular class of datatypes (such as *Time characteristics*) by clicking this button and selecting that class from its selection menu (H).

The base of the **Change Layout screen** contains the **Enter** and **Cancel buttons** (I). The function of the first button, which is to save your changes on the screen, can also be executed by hitting the **Enter key** on your keyboard. The function of the second button, which is to cancel your changes, can also be executed by clicking the control button in the upper-right corner of the screen.

> The **Summation column** is not always present in the **Columns window** of the **Change layout screen**. However, you can attach totals to columns on the main output screen, following the procedures described in the previous lesson.

Creating a Display Variant

The procedure for creating a display variant can be divided into two main tasks.

The first task, which is performed on the **Change Layout screen**, is to select those datatypes that you want to display in the line-item report, lay them out in their proper horizontal order, and attach totals to the bottoms of numerical data columns. The instructions for this task are provided in Steps 1 through 7 of the following procedure.

The second task, which is performed on the output screen, is to adjust the layout of the report (and specifically, the column widths) and filter, sort, group, and total its contents. The instructions for this task are given in Steps 8 and 9 of this next procedure.

Procedure

Creating a Display Variant for a Line-item Report

Step 1. Click the **Change layout** or **Current display variant button** in the application toolbar of the report screen (Figure 15.2B and Figure 15.3A), *or*

Follow the menu path **Settings > Layout > Change** (Figure 15.4).

Step 2. The **Change Layout screen** appears. Examine the list of the currently reported datatypes in the **Columns window** (Figure 15.6A), and transfer the unwanted ones to the **Column set window** (B) in one of these three ways.

- Double-click a datatype. This is the fastest way to transfer single datatypes.

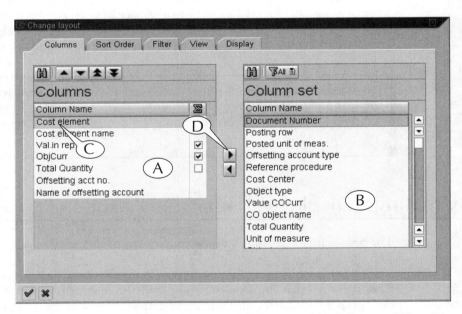

Figure 15.6   Select one or more unwanted datatypes in the **Columns window** (A), then move them to the **Column set window** (B) with the right-pointing control arrow (D).

- Click a datatype once to select and highlight it (C), then click the right-pointing control arrow (D) between the two windows.

- Click multiple datatypes while holding the **Ctrl key** on your keyboard to select and highlight them, then click the right-pointing control arrow (D) between the two windows.

For this example, we removed the **Cost element, ObjCurr, Total quantity, Offsetting account no.**, and **Name of offsetting account** datatypes from the **Columns window**, leaving behind only **Cost element name** and **Val in rep cur** (Figure 15.7).

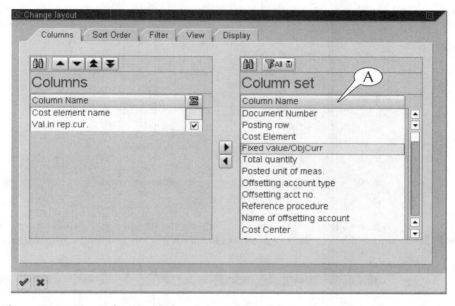

Figure 15.7 The **Columns window** is now free of the unwanted datatypes. Click the header (A) in the **Column Set window** to alphabetize the list of datatypes there.

Step 3. Click the **Column name header** (Figure 15.7A) in the **Column set window** to rearrange the listed datatypes. One click puts them in alphabetical order (Figure 15.8), and a second click puts them in reverse-alphabetical order. This step makes it easier to find datatypes in the window.

Step 4. Examine the list of available datatypes in the **Column set window**, and transfer the desired ones into the **Columns window** on the left by using the same three methods that were described in Step 2—but this time, use the *left-pointing* control arrow (Figure 15.8A) to transfer them.

For this example, we transferred these five datatypes: **User** (the business group code); **Name; Partner co code** (cost center code); **Document number**; and **Document header text** (Figure 15.9).

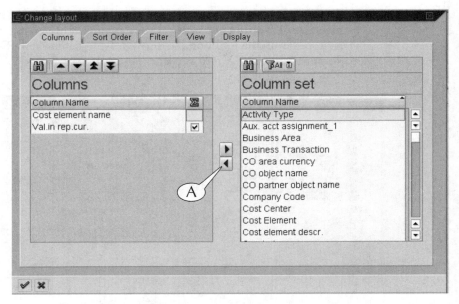

Figure 15.8   Select one or more desired datatypes in the **Column set window**, then move them to the **Columns window** with the left-pointing control arrow (A).

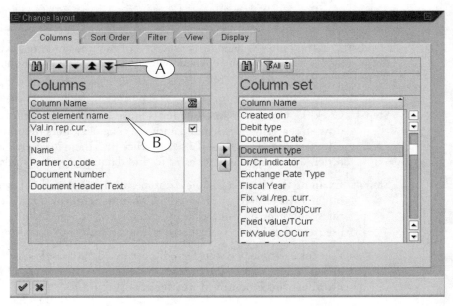

Figure 15.9   The desired datatypes are now in the **Columns window** and will appear in the display variant. Use the **positioning buttons** (A) to rearrange selected datatypes (B).

Step 5. Once you have the desired datatypes in the **Columns window**, rearrange them with the **positioning buttons** (Figure 15.9A). Their vertical order in the window corresponds to their horizontal order in the line-item report.

To rearrange the datatypes:

- Click a datatype to select and highlight it (Figure 15.9B), *or*

  Click several datatypes while you hold the **Ctrl key** on your keyboard to select and highlight them.

- Click one of the four **positioning buttons** to reposition the selected datatypes. The single-arrow buttons shift the positions of the datatypes up or down the list by one line, and the double-arrow buttons move them to the very top or bottom of the list.

Following are two guidelines to keep in mind when repositioning data columns during Step 5 of this procedure.

First, place logically related data columns together. For example, we put the employee name, number, and cost center columns next to each other in our report. We did the same for the document number and header text (Figure 15.10).

Second, if you plan to group and subgroup the line items in your report by one or more datatypes, place their columns on the left side of the report. For example, we plan to group the line items in our report by the cost element name, so we moved this datatype to the top of the list. If we had wanted to then subgroup them by a second datatype, we would have placed it second on the list.

Step 6. If you want to display totals for numerical data at the bottoms of their columns in the line-item report (and have that option on the screen), click their selection boxes (Figure 15.10A).

Step 7. You are now finished with the **Change Layout screen**. Click the **Enter key** (Figure 15.10B) to record your changes and return to the main output screen.

Step 8. The line-item report appears with the new datatypes in their proper order (Figure 15.11).

However, notice that the report is not laid out well: Some columns are so narrow that they cut off the display of their contents, and other columns are wider than they need to be. You can adjust the column widths in two ways.

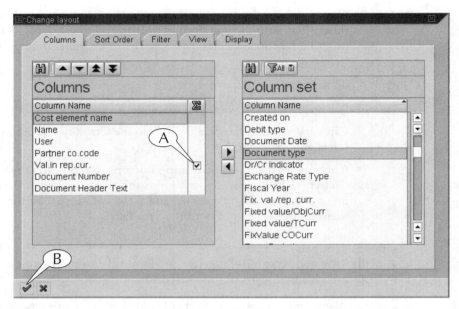

Figure 15.10   The datatypes are now arranged in a logical order. Use the selection boxes (A) in the **Summation column** to attach totals to numerical data columns.

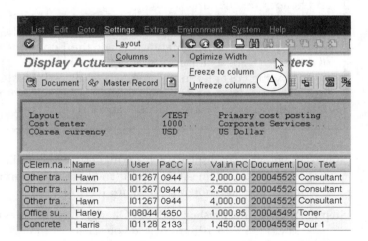

Figure 15.11   The line-item report returns with new datatypes in their proper order. Use the menu path to fix all the column widths at once.

- Adjust all the columns at once by following the menu path **Settings > Columns > Optimize Width** (Figure 15.11A). The system adjusts the width of all columns so that they fully display all their contents.

- Adjust the width of a single column by clicking-and-dragging its right header margin to a new position. As you click-and-drag the header margin, the cursor changes to a two-sided arrow (Figure 15.12A), and remains in that configuration until you release the margin.

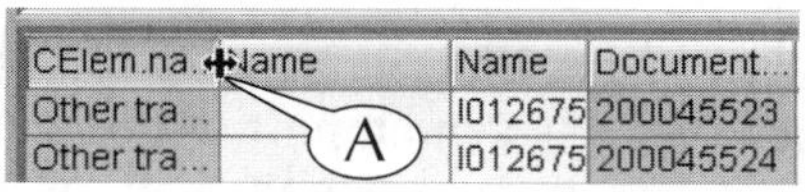

Figure 15.12   Fixing the column widths in the line-item report.

Step 9. Sort and group the line items in the report, add filters to edit their contents, and total and subtotal numerical data columns by following the procedures that were described in the previous lesson.

For this example, we grouped the line items by their cost element name and subtotaled the **Val in rep curr column** for each of the groups (Figure 15.13A).

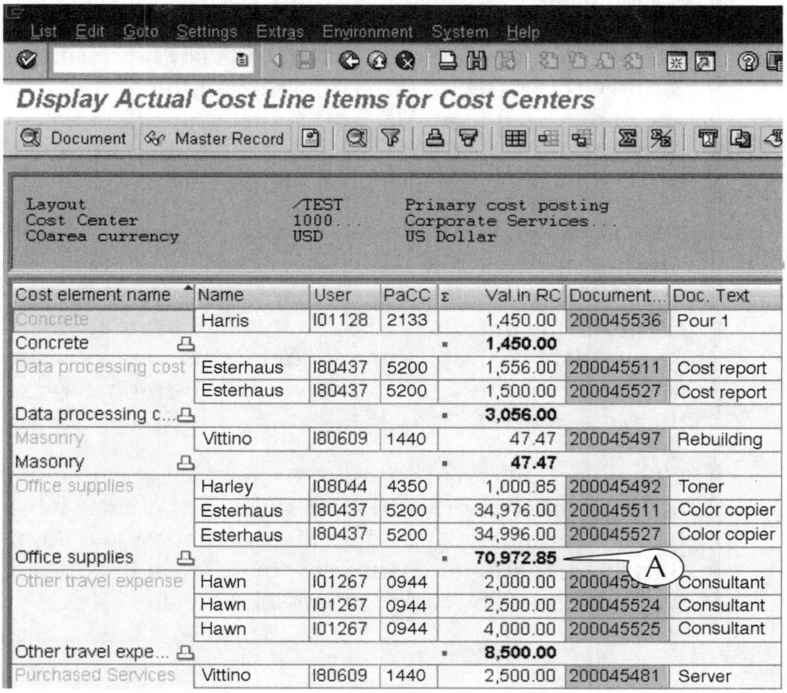

Figure 15.13   The display variant is now grouped by cost element name, and the groups are subtotaled (A). It is now finished.

End Procedure

This completes the procedure for creating a display variant. Where you once had a line-item report of dubious utility, you now have a report that shows the data you need to see, and only that data, in a well-organized layout (Figure 15.13).

This is the essence of a good report: It presents the *least* amount of data to convey the *most* amount of information. The data in our sample report—the cost element name, employee name, costs, and so on—are all needed to address the question: *Who spent our money on what?* There are no data in this report that do not address this question, for they would distract the reader from its message—and consume additional space while they did so.

We mentioned earlier that there are four other subscreens on the **Change Layout screen**, but we did not use them in this procedure. Frankly, we never use them when we are working with display variants, because their functions are more easily performed on the output screen itself.

For example, the **Sort order**, **Filter**, and **View subscreens** (Figure 15.14A, B, and C) could be used to sort and filter the data in a line-item report and convert it into an *MS Excel* spreadsheet. However, we prefer to perform such functions directly on the output screen, where we can see immediately the results of our effort.

The **Display subscreen** (Figure 15.14D) is perhaps the exception to this rule because it enables you to quickly remove row and column guidelines, column headings, and other features from a line-item report. However, the default settings on this screen are set to make the report very readable—the guidelines, for instance, help a reader follow a line of data across the screen—and we have never had reason to change them.

Of course, you can use these subscreens at any time if you prefer. The first two subscreens work exactly like the **Columns subscreen**—you transfer certain datatypes into the left window and then sort, sum, and filter them there—and you select or deselect the options on the other two subscreens by clicking their selection boxes.

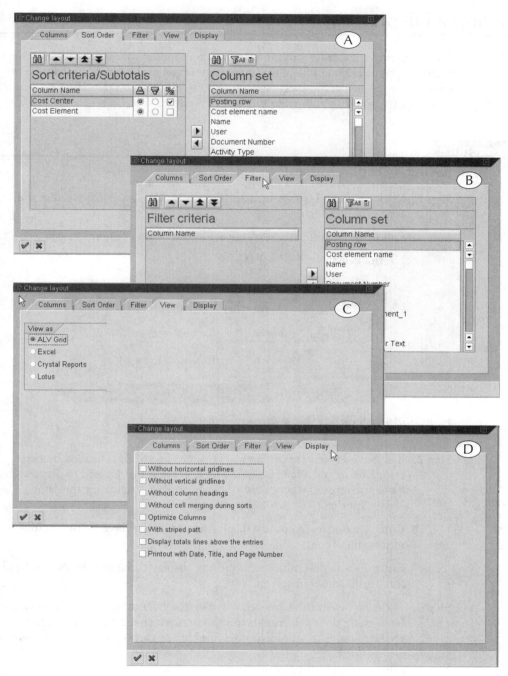

Figure 15.14   The four remaining subscreens of the **Change Layout screen**.

Saving a Display Variant

Once you create a display variant for a line-item report, you will probably want to use it whenever you execute this same transaction in the future so that you can compare the same data in successive reports. To do this, you must first save your new display variant by following the next procedure.

Procedure

Saving a Display Variant

Step 1. Click the **Save Layout button** (Figure 15.2D) if it is displayed in the application toolbar, *or*

Follow the menu path **Settings > Layout > Save** (Figure 15.15), *or*

Hit the keystroke **Ctrl + F10**.

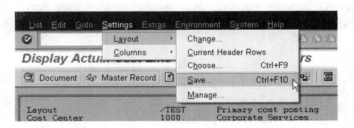

Figure 15.15 Menu path for saving a new display variant.

Step 2. The **Save layout screen** appears (Figure 15.16). It is headed by two tabs, *Save as* and *Save with* (A). The first tab is preselected to display the **Save subscreen**, where a list of other display variants for the same report appears (B).

- Enter a name for your new display variant in the **Save layout field** (C) of this subscreen.

- Enter a short description of your new display variant in the **Name field** (D) of this same subscreen.[1]

Step 3. *Optional:* Select the *User-specific option*, the *Default setting option*, or both by clicking their selection boxes (E) to place check marks inside them. (*Note:* Some SAP administrators disable one or both of these options.)

---

1. Yes, this field is wrongly named. Stuff happens, even in the best software.

- If you select the *User-specific option*, the new display variant is stored inside the desktop computer or workstation where it was created, and it can only be accessed by a user working at this machine.

  If you do not select this option, the new display variant is stored inside an SAP server, where it can be accessed by other users. This is a **global variant**, and a good way of sharing your variant with other users.

- If you select the *Default setting option*, the new display variant appears automatically whenever you run the same transaction in the future.

  If you do not select this option, the default variant appears whenever you run the same transaction in the future. To apply the new display variant in this case, you must call it up with one of the next two procedures.

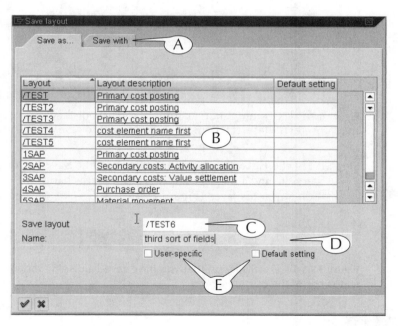

Figure 15.16   Enter a name (C) and description (D) of the new display variant on the **Save subscreen**, and select from the options at its bottom (E).

Step 4. *Optional*: Click the second tab to display the **Save with subscreen** (Figure 15.17). This subscreen lists other customization features that you applied to the display variant, including filters and sorts. They are preselected, and they will be saved as a permanent part of the variant unless you deselect them.

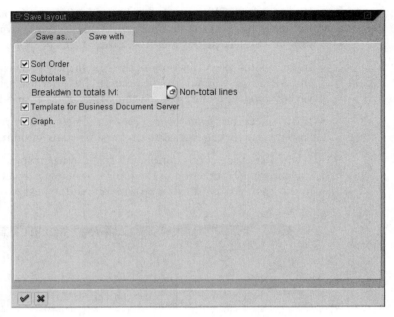

Figure 15.17   Customization features of the new display variant are indicated on this subscreen. Deselect them if you don't want to save them with the variant.

Step 5.   Hit the **Enter key** on your keyboard. The **Save Layout screen** is erased, and a message appears in the status bar of the output screen that the variant is saved (Figure 15.18).

Figure 15.18   Confirmation that you have saved a display variant appears in the status bar of the output screen.

End Procedure

Applying a Display Variant

You have the option of saving a display variant in default mode so that it is applied automatically to the line-item whenever you execute the same transaction.

However, it is common for users to create more than one display variant for a given transaction. For example, we maintain several display variants for the line-item report of the *KSB1 transaction*, including the variant that we set up in the first procedure in this lesson and a second variant that reports accounting data (when we need to discuss our costs with our bookkeeper). Consequently, we did not identify a default display variant for the transaction. Rather, we apply one of our several variants on an *ad hoc* basis, depending on our specific needs at the moment.

There are two ways to apply a display variant in this way. We describe them as *before-the-fact* and *after-the-fact applications*.

You can apply a display variant *before the fact*—that is, before you execute the transaction—if its initial screen contains the **Layout field**[2] (Figure 15.19A). When it does, enter the name of the variant there and execute the transaction, and the line-item report appears automatically in the format of that variant. (If you don't remember its name, click the search button (B) of the field to call up a hit list of the available display variants for the transaction.)

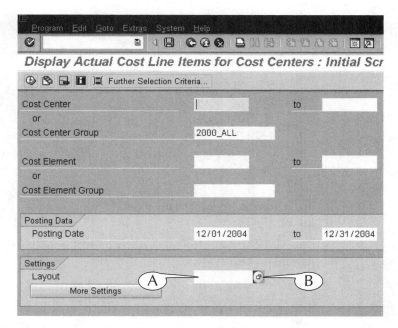

Figure 15.19   You can often enter the names of display variants in the **Layout field** of the initial screens of many list-display transactions.

_____

2. This screen element is not always found on the initial screens of transactions that allow display variants.

When the initial screen of the transaction does not contain the **Layout field** or if you forget to enter the name of the display variant there before you execute the transaction, you can apply it *after the fact*—that is, after a transaction is executed and the line-item report appears in its default format—by following this next procedure.

Procedure

Applying a Display Variant After the Fact

Step 1. Click the **Choose** *or* **Get button** (Figure 15.2C) in the application toolbar of the output screen, *or*

Follow the menu path **Settings > Layout > Choose** *or* **Get** (Figure 15.20), *or*

Hit the keystroke **Ctrl + F9**.

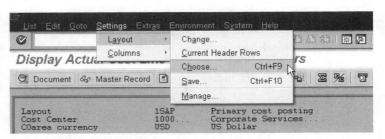

Figure 15.20   Menu path for applying a display variant to a line-item report after the fact.

Step 2. The **Choose layout screen** appears with a list of available variants (Figure 15.21).

- *Optional:* Rearrange the list in order of the layout description by clicking its column header.

- Locate the desired variant and double-click its line.

Step 3. The line-item report is reformatted in the style of the selected variant.

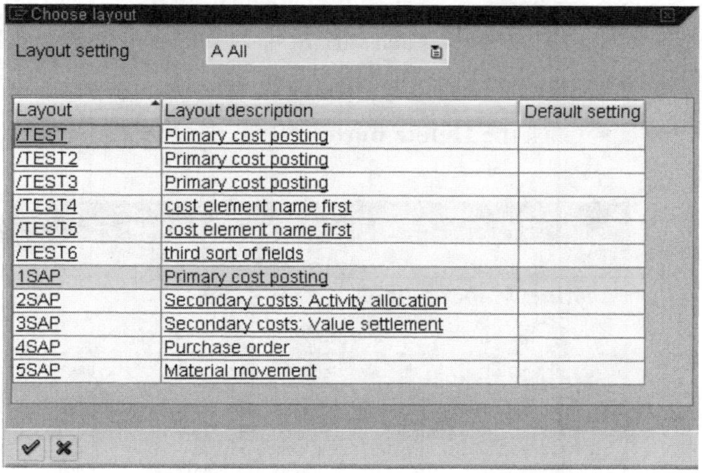

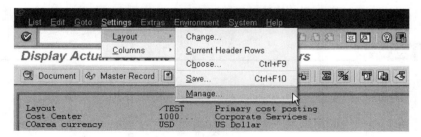

Figure 15.21 Select the display variant from this screen.

End Procedure

Deleting a Display Variant

You may very well accumulate a collection of display variants over time as you use the system and your job function changes. You should "clean house" on occasion and get rid of out-of-date variants by following this next procedure.

Procedure

Deleting a Display Variant

Step 1. Follow the menu path **Settings > Layout > Administration** *or* **Manage** *or* **Management** (Figure 15.22).

Figure 15.22 Menu path for deleting a display variant.

Step 2. The **Layout: Management screen** appears with a list of available display variants. Each variant has a selection box to its left (Figure 15.23A).

- Select a variant by clicking its selection box.
- Click the **Delete button** (B) in the application toolbar.

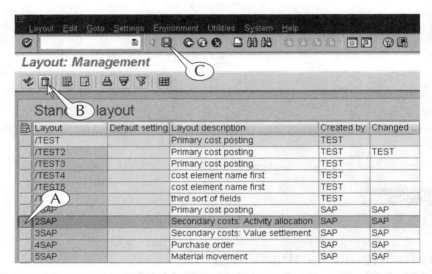

Figure 15.23 Select the display variant to delete (A), click the **Delete button** (B), then click the **Save button** (C) to return to the output screen.

Step 3. The display variant is erased from the list.

- Click the **Save button** (C) to record your changes and return to the output screen, where confirmation of your action appears in the status bar (Figure 15.24).

Figure 15.24 Confirmation that you deleted a display variant appears in the status bar of the output screen.

End Procedure

Working With Display Variants on Other Screens

We described the various procedures for using display variants on the output screens of *list-display transactions* throughout this lesson. However, you can also apply the same procedures to the line-item tables that you will find on the initial and output screens of other transactions.

For example, the initial screen for the *ME51N transaction*, which creates requisitions for materials and services, contains a line-item table (A) for entering data about those requisitions (Figure 15.25). The output screen for the *ME53N transaction*, which displays requisition data, contains this same table in a read-only format. Each line of these tables contains data for one requisitioned material item or service, which are entered in a long series of columns. To see all these data, you must scroll horizontally along the length of the table.

However, it is possible to create a display variant for this table with fewer columns. The procedure begins at the **Layout Settings button** (B) in the application toolbar of the table. Click this button to display a list of variant-related commands, then follow the same procedures that we offered in the earlier part of this lesson.

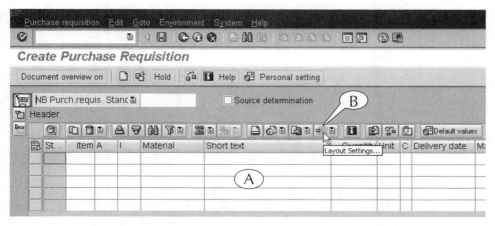

Figure 15.25   The initial screen for creating a requisition contains a line-item table. You can create and work with variants for this table with the commands of the **Layout Settings button** (B).

Lesson 16

EXPORTING LINE-ITEM REPORTS TO MICROSOFT EXCEL AND WORD

The previous lessons described the procedures for customizing line-item reports with various tools that are available in SAP. But thanks to a strategic alliance between SAP and Microsoft, it is also possible to convert SAP line-item reports into *Excel* spreadsheets and *Word* documents (where you can then use the tools of these powerful applications to customize them) or into unformatted data (which can easily be pasted into an e-mail message).

There are two classes of methods for exporting SAP line-item reports to these applications. For the lack of better names, we call them **front-door exports** and **back-door exports**.

- Front-door exports use menu paths and tool buttons in the application toolbars of output screens to automatically convert reports into fully formatted *Excel* spreadsheets and *Word* documents.

- Back-door exports simply "dump" raw unformatted SAP data into an external storage location, such as the hard drive on your personal computer. You must then convert them into Microsoft spreadsheets and documents by executing several additional steps.

This lesson describes the procedures for exporting SAP line-item reports to these applications, and specifically into *MS Excel*. We limit this discussion to *MS Excel* for three reasons.

- Converting SAP line-item reports into *MS Excel* spreadsheets is by far the most common and obvious use of the export tool, and some output screens are set up exclusively for this purpose.

- SAP line-item reports are converted into tables when they are exported into *MS Word*. *Excel* is the better tool for working with tables.

- The procedures for exporting SAP reports to *MS Word* are exactly the same as those for exporting them to *MS Excel*.

However, we also make mention of the means of exporting SAP reports to *MS Word* whenever it is appropriate.

We should also note that we only describe the procedures for exporting SAP line-item reports to *Excel* in this lesson. We do not describe the procedures for customizing them once they arrive there: You will have to buy another book to learn about that!

Front-Door Exports

We describe here two procedures for front-door exports of SAP line-item reports to *MS Excel.*

This first procedure can be executed whenever you find the **Option/Office Integration button** in the application toolbar of the output screen of a line-item report (Figure 16.1A). This button enables you to instantly convert the report into an *Excel* spreadsheet, but not a *Word* document.

We demonstrate this first procedure with the output of the *Cost Center Actual/Plan/Variance transaction*. This transaction displays the budget of a department (or *cost center*) in a business or an organization in line-item format (Figure 16.1). Each line of the report shows, for a single cost category or *cost element*, the actual and planned costs and the difference or *variance* between them.

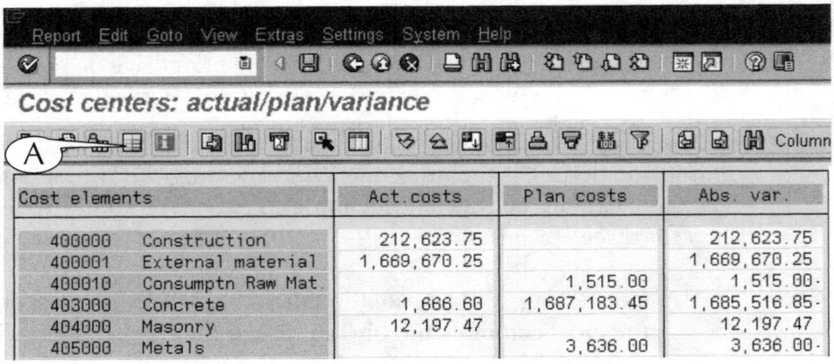
Report Edit Goto View Extras Settings System Help
Cost centers: actual/plan/variance
Column
A
Cost elements
Act.costs
Plan costs
Abs. var.
400000 Construction 212,623.75 212,623.75
400001 External material 1,669,670.25 1,669,670.25
400010 Consumptn Raw Mat. 1,515.00 1,515.00-
403000 Concrete 1,666.60 1,687,183.45 1,685,516.85-
404000 Masonry 12,197.47 12,197.47
405000 Metals 3,636.00 3,636.00-

Figure 16.1 Use the **Option/Office Integration button** to call up the **Options screen.**

Procedure

Exporting to *MS Excel* With the Option/Office Integration Button

Step 1. Click the **Option/Office Integration button** (Figure 16.1A) in the application toolbar of the output screen.

Step 2. The **Options screen** appears (Figure 16.2). The screen is divided into four field areas. The lowest one, *Office Integration*, contains three radio buttons for controlling the format of the report.

- *Inactive*, the default setting, displays the report in SAP format.

- *Microsoft Excel* displays the report as an *Excel* spreadsheet.

- *Lotus 123* displays the report as a *Lotus* spreadsheet.

  Select the *Microsoft Excel option* (A).

Step 3. *Optional:* Select the *Worksheet protection option* (B) to create a read-only *Excel* spreadsheet.

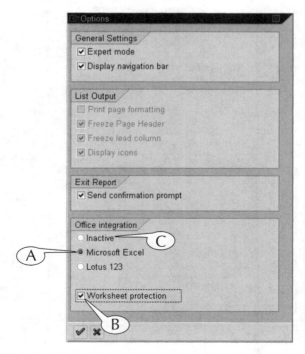

Figure 16.2   Click the *Microsoft Excel option* to convert the line-item report into an *Excel* spreadsheet.

Step 4. Hit the **Enter key** on your keyboard, and the line-item report is reformatted as an *Excel* spreadsheet (Figure 16.3).

This spreadsheet appears inside an *MS Excel* application window that is itself embedded inside the SAP session. However, the *Excel* application window is fully functional: It possesses all the menus, tools, tabs, and other features that are associated with this software.

Step 5. Save the spreadsheet in an external storage location by

- Following the menu path **File > Save as** in the menu bar of the *Excel* application window, *or*

Clicking the **Save button** (A) in its toolbar.

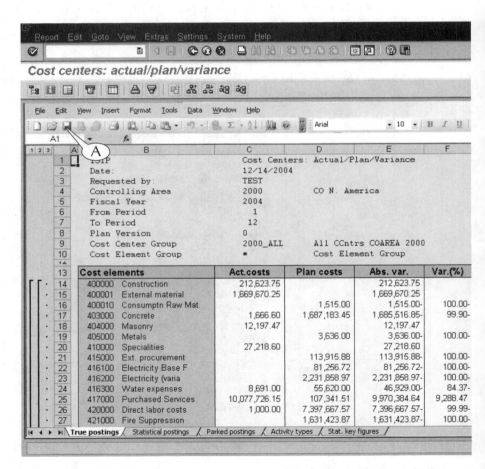

Figure 16.3 The spreadsheet appears in an *Excel* application window, which is embedded inside the SAP window.

To convert the spreadsheet back into SAP format, recall the **Options screen** and select the *Inactive option* (Figure 16.2C) from the **Office Integration field area**.

You can use this second procedure whenever you find the **List Export menu** in the menu bar of the output screen of line-item reports. This menu contains two commands, *Spreadsheet* and *Word Processing*, for exporting a report to *MS Excel* and *Word* (Figure 16.4A). You may also find buttons in the application toolbar of some (but not all) screens for executing these same commands (Figure 16.4B and C).

We demonstrate this second procedure with the output of the *KSBI transaction* (Figure 16.4). This transaction displays the expenditures or *actual costs* for a department (or *cost center*) in a business or an organization in a line-item format.

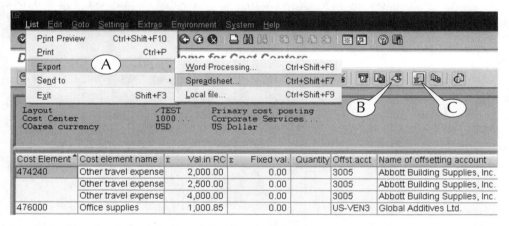

Figure 16.4   Use the *Spreadsheet* and *Word Processing* menu commands (A) or the **Word Processing** (B) and **Spreadsheet** (C) **buttons** to export line-item reports.

Procedure

Exporting to *MS Excel* With the List Menu

Step 1.   Follow the menu path **List > Export > Spreadsheet** (Figure 16.4A), *or*

Click the **Spreadsheet button** (C) in the application toolbar (if it is there).

Step 2. A popup screen with the same title as the output screen appears to inform you that any filters, sorts, and sums that you added to the report will not be carried over into the *Excel* spreadsheet (Figure 16.5).

- Hit the **Enter key** on your keyboard.

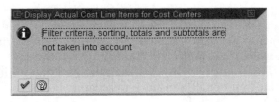

Figure 16.5   Just hit the **Enter key** to continue past this popup screen.

Step 3. The **Export list object to XXL screen** appears with radio buttons for three alternative export options (Figure 16.6).

- Select the *Table option* (A) to create a normal spreadsheet. You also have the option of creating a pivot table.

- Hit the **Enter key** on your keyboard.

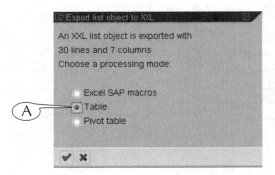

Figure 16.6   Select either the *Table (or Pivot table) option* for a spreadsheet.

Step 4. A second **Export list object to XXL screen** appears with the *Microsoft Excel option*, which is already selected for you (Figure 16.7).

- Hit the **Enter key** on your keyboard.

Figure 16.7   No choice on this screen, so hit the **Enter key** on your keyboard.

Step 5. The spreadsheet appears in an *MS Excel* application window, which
opens outside the SAP application window (Figure 16.8).

   ■ Save the spreadsheet in the usual way.

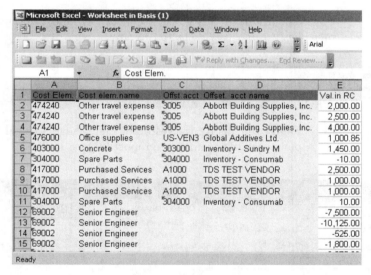

Figure 16.8   The spreadsheet appears in its own application window.

End Procedure

Back-Door Exports

You can export line-item reports to *MS Excel* and *Word* with a convenient "back door" command in the **System menu**. You can use this method on any output screens with line-item reports, but it is a particularly handy tool for search hit list screens and other output screens that do not have the **Option/Office Integration button** in their application toolbars or the **List menu** in their menu bars. In addition, this tool creates a file that is considerably smaller than an *Excel* or a *Word* file, and thus easier to e-mail to other users.

This procedure is slightly longer than front-door exports because it involves two separate phases. First, you export the data in the line-item report to an external storage location, where it is stored in a *comma-separated values (csv)* formatted file. Once this is done, you must call up the file in *Excel* or *Word* and reformat it there.

We again demonstrate this procedure by exporting the output of the *Cost Center Actual/Plan/Variance transaction* to *MS Excel*.

Procedure

Back-Door Export of a Line-item Report to *MS Excel*

Step 1. Follow the menu path **System > List > Save > Local file** (A) on the output screen of the line-item report (Figure 16.9).

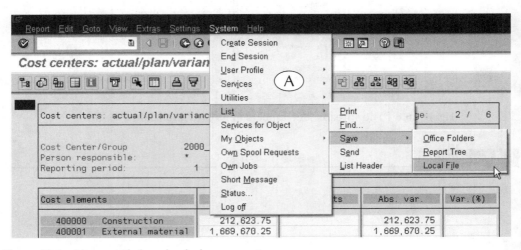

Figure 16.9 Menu path for a back-door export.

Step 2. The **Save List in File screen** appears with five selection options (Figure 16.10).

- Select the *Spreadsheet option* (A).
- Hit the **Enter key** on your keyboard.

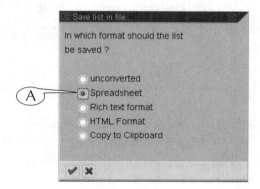

Figure 16.10 Select *Spreadsheet* to create a raw csv file with the report data.

Step 3. The **Save as screen** for the *Windows* operating system (or the equivalent screen for another operating system) appears (Figure 16.11).

- Select an external storage location in the **Save in field** (A).
- Enter a name for the raw data file in the **File name field** (B), followed by the file extension *.xls (dot xls)*.
- Check that the entry in the **Save as type field** (C) reads *EXCEL Files (*.XLS)*. If it is not correct, change it.
- Hit the **Save button** (D) to save the file, which is stored in csv format.

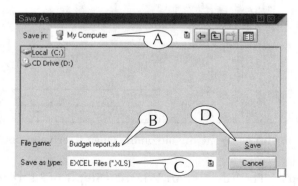

Figure 16.11 Save the file with the *.xls* extension.

Step 4. Boot up the *MS Excel* application on your computer in the usual way.

Step 5. Follow the menu path **File > Open** (A) in the menu bar of the application, or click the **Open button** in its standard toolbar (Figure 16.12).

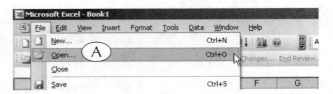

Figure 16.12   Boot up *Excel*, then open the file through the menu bar or toolbar.

Step 6. The **Open screen** for the *Windows* operating system (or the equivalent screen for another operating system) appears (Figure 16.13).

- Locate the exported file in your external storage location, and double-click its name or icon to open it.

    Note: If you forget to add the *.xls* extension to the file name in Step 3, you won't see the file because the screen is set to display only *Excel* files (A). Change the entry in the **Files of type field** to *All files* and you will then see it.

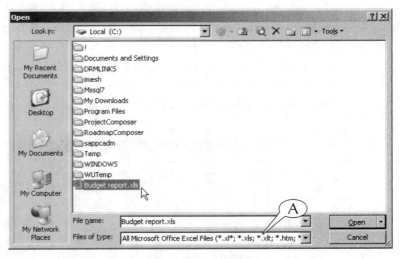

Figure 16.13   Locate the file on the **Open screen** and double-click it.

Step 7. The **Text Import Wizard - Step 1 of 3 screen** appears (Figure 16.14).

- Click the **Finish button** (A).

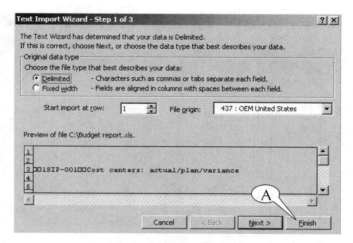

Figure 16.14   No need to go through all three steps on the **Text Import Wizard screen**: just click the **Finish button** (A).

Step 8.   A properly formatted spreadsheet appears in an *MS Excel* application window, which opens outside the SAP application window.

- Reformat and save the spreadsheet in the usual way.

End Procedure

Incidentally, you can use this procedure to export the hit lists of search screens to *MS Excel* and *Word* with one small change to the previous procedure.

This change comes in Step 1 because hit lists do not have menu bars. Rather, right-click the hit list to call up a shortcut menu (Figure 16.15A), then scroll down and select the *Download command* at its very bottom. Continue the procedure at Step 2.

> To export a line-item report to *MS Word* through the back door:
>
> 1. Select either the *Rich text* or *HTML format* in Step 2.
> - *Rich text format* exports the reports to *MS Word* in that format, which is the raw material for creating *Word* text documents.
> - *HTML format* exports the report to *MS Word* in that format, which is the raw material for creating Web pages.
> 2. Save the file with the extension *.rtf* or *.html* in Step 3.
> 3. Boot up *Word* in Step 4.

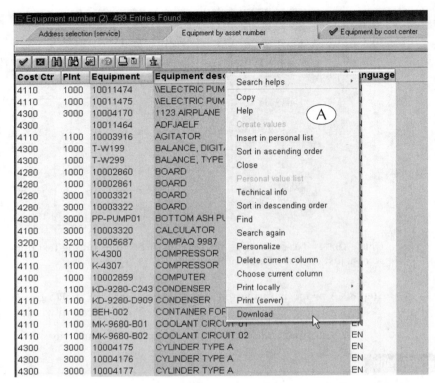

Figure 16.15   Right-click a hit list to call up a shortcut menu, and select the *Download command* as Step 1 of the back-door export.

Lesson 17

SENDING LINE-ITEM REPORTS VIA SAP E-MAIL

Once you generate a line-item report with a list-display transaction, you may want to share it with other people in your company or organization. Of course, you could always print the report by clicking the **Print button** in the standard toolbar of the output screen (Figure 17.1A) so that you can manually distribute the hard copy to the interested parties. You could also export the report to *MS Excel*, and then e-mail it to them as an attachment with *MS Outlook* or another e-mail application.

However, SAP has its own e-mail application that you can use to send line-item reports, messages, and other documents to other users of the system. You can start this process from the output screen of any line-item report in one of two ways.

- Click the **Mail recipient button** (B) in the application toolbar, *or*

  Follow the menu path **List > Send to > Mail recipient** *or* **List > Save > Office** (depending on the module).

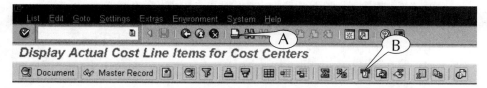

Figure 17.1   You can access the SAP e-mail application through the menu bar or the application toolbar.

This action calls up the **Create and Send Document screen** (Figure 17.2) on which you can address the e-mail to its recipients, add a cover letter and attach other documents to it, and send the report. The recipients receive and read your e-mail and its attachments in their **Business Workplace**, where they can also store them and send e-mail to other users.

This lesson describes the procedures for sending and receiving line-item reports (along with other messages and documents) with the SAP e-mail application. It also introduces you to the **Business Workplace**, where you can send, receive, and store e-mail with this application.

The Create Document and Send Screen

The **Create Document and Send screen** (Figure 17.2) appears when you click the **Mail recipient button** (Figure 17.1B) or follow the appropriate menu path on the output screen of a list-display transaction.

This screen contains two subscreens in which you can create a cover letter, attach other documents to the e-mail, define its properties, and enter the names of one or more recipients. The subscreens are overlain by the **Title field** (Figure 17.2A), in which you can enter a title or description for the message and its contents.

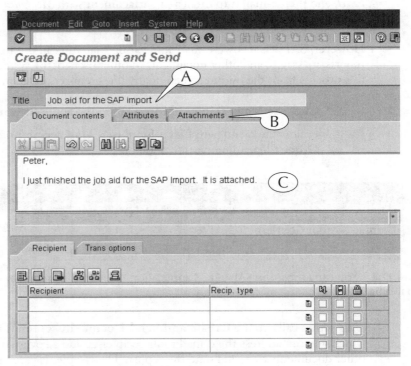

Figure 17.2 Entering a title (A) and a cover letter (C) for the e-mail.

The Upper Subscreen

The display of the upper subscreen of the **Create Document and Send screen** is controlled by three tabs: *Document contents*, *Attributes*, and *Attachments* (Figure 17.2B). The first tab is selected by default when the screen appears.

The **Document content subscreen** contains a text field in which you can enter a cover letter to its recipient (Figure 17.2C). The use of this text field is optional.

The **Attributes subscreen** contains seven data fields, in which the e-mail and its attached documents are described (Figure 17.3A). The first two, **Document class** and **Document size**, appear in the gray read-only mode. The first describes the attached document as either *SAP Editor Document* (if it is a line-item report) or *PC Document* (if it was created by a desktop application such as *Excel* or *Adobe Acrobat*). The second field describes the document size in bytes.

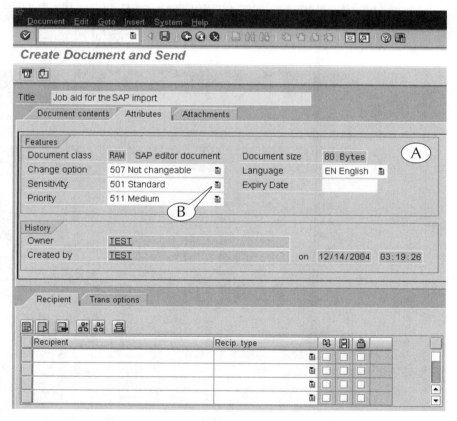

Figure 17.3   Setting the attributes of the e-mail and its attachments.

The remaining five fields of the **Attributes subscreen** contain **list icons** (B), which you can click to display and select from a drop-down menu of optional entries.

- **Change option**: by which the sender can set the attached document as *Changeable* by any user; *Changeable* by the author only; or *Not changeable* by any user

- **Language**: which is usually set by default by the SAP administrator

- **Sensitivity**: by which the sender can describe the attached document as *Standard* (not sensitive) or *Confidential* (readable only by the recipient)

- **Expiry date**: by which the sender can set a date on which the message is deleted automatically if it has not been read by its recipients

- **Priority**: which can be defined as *Low*, *Medium*, or *High*

The **Attachments subscreen** provides a description of the attached document, including its size and type (Figure 17.4A). This subscreen also has its own application toolbar, which contains three especially useful buttons.

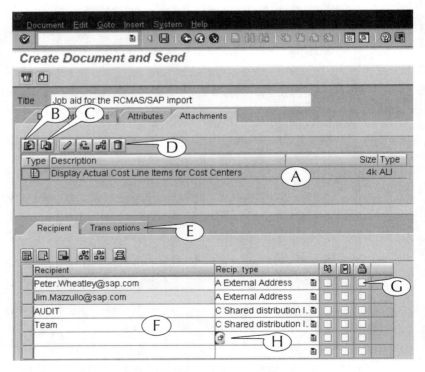

Figure 17.4   Working with the attachments to e-mail.

- The **Create attachment button** (B) enables you to attach other documents from an external storage location, such as the hard drive of your personal computer, to the e-mail. Simply click it to call up the **Import file screen** of the *Windows* operating system (Figure 17.5A), locate the document, and double-click its name to attach it.

- The **Export attachment button** (C) enables you to store a copy of a document in an external location. Simply click the document line to select and highlight it, then click the button to call up the **Export file screen** of the *Windows* operating system (Figure 17.5B), on which you can name and store the document.

- The **Delete button** (D) enables you to delete an attached document from the e-mail. Simply click the document line to select and highlight it, then click this button.

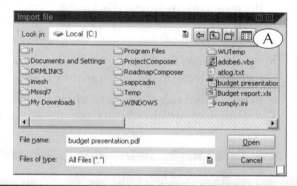

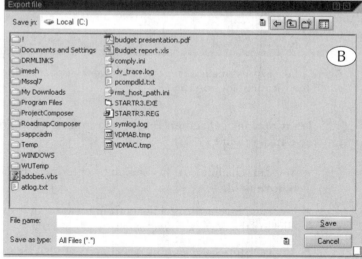

Figure 17.5   Select a new attachment from the **Import file screen** (A), or store an attachment in an external site using the **Export file screen** (B).

The Lower Subscreen

The display of the lower subscreen of the **Create Document and Send screen** is controlled by two tabs: **Recipient** and **Trans options** (Figure 17.4E). The first tab is selected by default when the screen appears.

The **Recipient subscreen** contains a line-item table for entering data about the recipients of the e-mail. You can enter the names of single recipients and the names of **distribution lists** of multiple recipients in its **Recipient column** (F) by following the procedures in the next two sections of this lesson.

Each line of this subscreen also contains three selection boxes (G). From left to right, they are:

- **Express mail**: Sends a message to a recipient that an e-mail is waiting in the recipient's **Business Workplace**. This message is flashed on the screen when the recipient logs on to SAP (Figure 17.6). To read the e-mail, the recipient would click the **Execute button** on this screen (A).

- **Send as copy**: Sends a copy of the e-mail to a recipient, and lists the recipient's name in the header of the e-mail for all other recipients to see.

- **Send as blind copy**: Sends a blind copy of the e-mail to a recipient, so that the blind-copy recipient's name does not appear in the header of the e-mail.

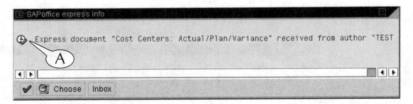

Figure 17.6   Express mail causes this message to appear on the recipient's monitor when the recipient logs on to SAP.

The **Trans options subscreen** enables you to set the conditions for transmitting the e-mail (Figure 17.7A).

- You can schedule its transmission by entering a date in the **Do not send before field**.

- You can prevent the recipients from forwarding it to other users by clicking the *No forwarding option*.

- You can store a copy of the e-mail in your own **Business Workplace** by selecting the *After sending, move to outbox option*.

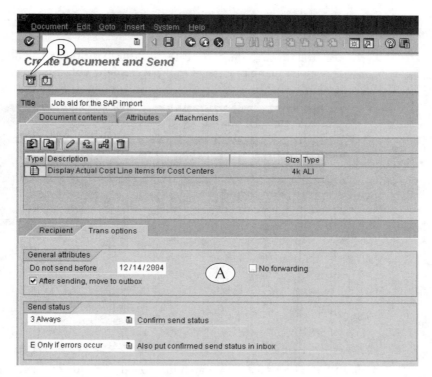

Figure 17.7   Setting the conditions for transmitting the e-mail.

Once you enter messages, attach documents, and select options on these five subscreens, you can send your e-mail by clicking the **Send mail button** (Figure 17.7B), which can be found in the application toolbar *and* at the bottom of the **Create Document and Send screen**.

Entering and Searching for the Names of Recipients

You can enter the names of individual recipients on the **Recipients subscreen** by entering their first or last name in the first available field of the **Recipient column** (Figure 17.4F), then hitting the **Enter key** on your keyboard. One of two things will then happen.

- If there is one user of your system with that name, the system automatically enters that user's full name in the field.

- If there is more than one user with that name, the **Address management: Find contact person hit list screen** appears with all their first and last names, as well as their affiliations and telephone numbers (Figure 17.8).

Scroll through the list, locate the desired recipient, and double-click that person's name to enter it in the **Recipient column**.

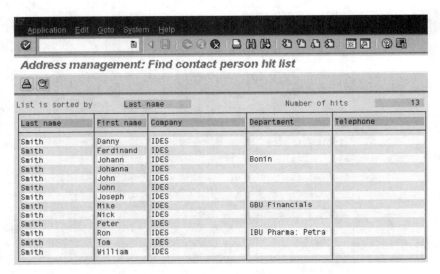

Figure 17.8   The hit list for a search for individual recipients of an e-mail.

If you are not certain of the name of the recipient, you can search for it by this next procedure.[1]

Procedure

Searching for Recipients

Step 1. Click inside the first available field in the **Recipient column** to call up its search button (Figure 17.4H), then click it.

Step 2. The **Selection screen** appears with radio buttons for several recipient types (Figure 17.9). The *Internal User option* (A) is selected by default.

- ▪ Enter the last name of the recipient in the **Srch field** (B). (You can also enter a first name, but this will probably result in a very long hit list, unless that first name is not a common one.)

- ▪ Click the **Detailed search button** (C) at the bottom of the screen.

---

1. See Lesson 10 for a complete description of search procedures.

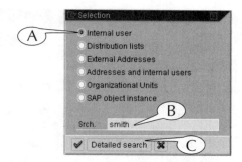

Figure 17.9   Searching for the correct name of an individual recipient.

Step 3. The **Address management: Find contact person hit list screen** appears with a list of matches to your search criteria (Figure 17.8).

Scroll through the list, locate the correct recipient, and double-click the person's name to enter it in the **Recipient column**.

End Procedure

Working With Distribution Lists

Distribution lists are lists of multiple recipients for e-mail messages. You can create such lists by following this next procedure.

Procedure

Creating Distribution Lists

Step 1. Enter the names of all the members of the new list in the **Recipient column** of the **Recipients subscreen** (Figure 17.10A).

Step 2. Click the selection boxes (B) of all the individuals you want to include on this list to select and highlight them. You can select all the names on the subscreen by clicking the **Select all button** (C) in its application toolbar.

Step 3. Click the **Create dist button** (D) in the application toolbar.

Step 4. The **Create Distribution List Header screen** appears (Figure 17.11).

- Enter a name for the new list in the **Name field** (A).
- Enter a description for the new list in the **Title field** (B).
- Hit the **Enter key** on your keyboard.

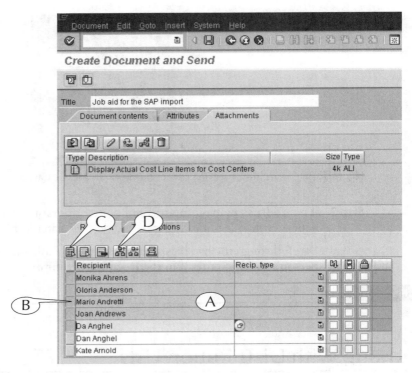

Figure 17.10   Enter the names of all the members of the new distribution list here.

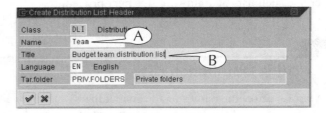

Figure 17.11   Name the new distribution list here.

Step 5.   A message appears in the status bar of the **Create Document and Send screen** that the list is created (Figure 17.12).

Figure 17.12   Confirmation that the distribution list is created comes in the status bar of the **Create Document and Send screen**.

End Procedure

You can enter the names of **distribution lists** in the **Recipient column** by following the same procedure for entering the names of recipients. For example, if you know the exact name of the list, enter it in the first available field of the **Recipient column** and hit the **Enter key** on your keyboard. If you don't know the exact name of the list, follow this next procedure.

Searching for Distribution Lists

Step 1. Click inside the first available field in the **Recipient column** to call up its search button (Figure 17.4H), then click it.

Step 2. The **Selection screen** appears with radio buttons for several recipient types (Figure 17.13).

- Select the *Distribution lists option* (A).
- Click the **Detailed search button** (B) at the bottom of the screen.

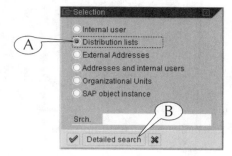

Figure 17.13 Select the *Distribution list option* to search for lists.

Step 3. The **Selection Criteria for Distribution Lists screen** appears (Figure 17.14).

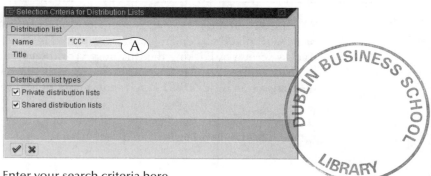

Figure 17.14 Enter your search criteria here.

- Enter part of the name of the list, preceded and followed by asterisks (*), in the **Name field** (A).

- Hit the **Enter key** on your keyboard.

Step 4. If there is only one match to your selection criteria, it is automatically entered in the **Recipient column**.

If there are multiple matches to your criteria, the **Selection Distribution Lists screen** appears (Figure 17.15). Locate the desired list(s).

- Double-click the name of one list, and it is entered in the column.

- Click the selection boxes (A) of several lists to select and highlight them, then hit the **Enter key** on your keyboard to enter them in the column.

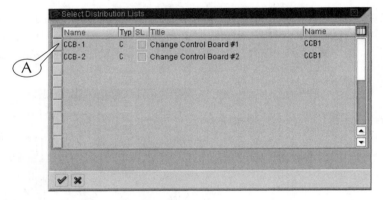

Figure 17.15   Hit list for a distribution list search.

End Procedure

Reading SAP E-mail Messages

SAP e-mail and their attached documents can be read and managed on the **Business Workplace screen**. You can navigate to that screen from the **SAP Easy Access screen** by clicking the **Business Workplace button** in its application toolbar (Figure 17.16A). You can also navigate there from *any* screen by entering the transaction code */nSBWP* in its **command field** (B).

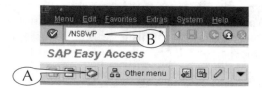

Figure 17.16   Navigating to the **Business Workplace screen** via the application toolbar (on the **SAP Easy Access screen** only) or the command field (on any screen).

The **Business Workplace screen** has the same general design as other screens in the SAP system (Figure 17.17). For instance, it has a menu bar, standard toolbar, title bar (which displays your name), and an application toolbar at its top; a status bar for messages and warnings at its base; and a central work area between them. The key difference is the design of its central work area: It is divided into the **folder** (A), **contents** (B) and **preview** (C) **panels**, which are separated by **panes** (D). You can adjust the sizes and shapes of the three panels by clicking-and-dragging these panes into new positions.

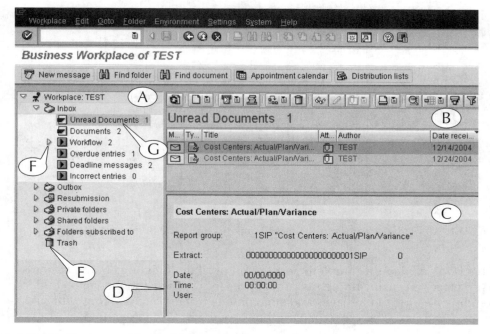

Figure 17.17   Elements of the **Business Workplace screen**.

The **Business Workplace screen** serves many different functions for its users. However, we limit our discussion in this lesson to its use for sending, receiving, and storing e-mail messages, which is the most frequent use of this screen by most users of the system.

Why? The simple reason is that we could write a whole book about this screen and its functions—except that there is already such a book, which you can download from this screen by clicking the **Customizing of local layout button** (Figure 17.18A) in its application toolbar and selecting the *SAP GUI help command* (B).

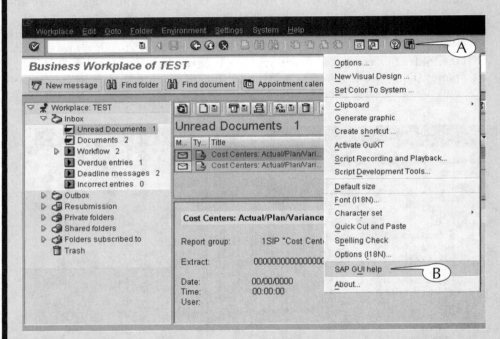

Figure 17.18 Downloading a free manual for working in the **Business Workplace**.

That book contains a complete description of all the functions of the **Business Workplace screen**, including the procedures for creating and managing folders, sending all sorts of messages and attachments from it, and working with substitutes. It is an excellent resource for the "heavy users" of this screen.

The **folder panel** contains several subfolders for storing your incoming and out-going e-mail, and a **trash bin** (Figure 17.17E) for deleted e-mail. Each folder usually contains several subfolders, which you can display or hide by clicking the control arrows (F) to the left of their names.

Incoming e-mail is automatically stored by the system in the **Unread Documents subfolder** (G) of the **Inbox folder**. The number of unread e-mail messages is indicated to the right of the subfolder name. To display and read e-mail, follow this next procedure.

Procedure

Reading E-mail in the Business Workplace

Step 1. Open the **Inbox folder** and click the **Unread Documents subfolder** to select and highlight it (Figure 17.17G).

Step 2. The e-mail in the subfolder appears in a line-item table in the **contents panel** (B). Each line displays the title, attributes, source, and date of one e-mail.

To read the cover letter of an e-mail, click its name to select and high-light it, and the letter is displayed in the **preview panel** (C).

Step 3. To access the entire e-mail, including its attached documents, double-click its name in the **contents panel** (B).

Step 4. The **Display Document [Title] screen** for the e-mail appears (Figure 17.19). It contains tabs (A) near its top for displaying four subscreens. The **Doc contents subscreen** is selected by default, and displays the cover letter of the e-mail (if there is one) and links (B) to the attached documents.

- To display an attached document, double-click its link. A second application window appears with a display of that document. If the attachment is an SAP data output screen, you will be able to read that screen, but not drill down into it.

Step 5. Once you read the e-mail and its attached documents, do the following.

- Close the application window of the document.

- *Optional:* Reply to the e-mail or forward it to another user. (See the procedures at the end of this lesson.)

- Click the **Back button** (Figure 17.19C) in the standard toolbar of the **Display Document [Title] screen** to return to the **Business Work-place screen**.

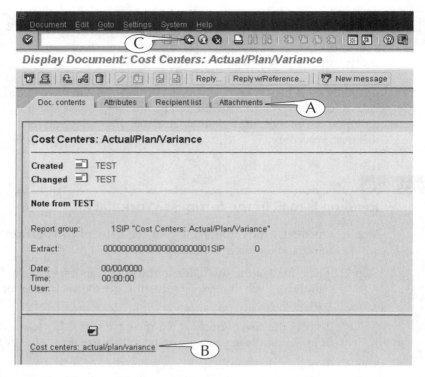

Figure 17.19 Display of the cover letter and attachment of an e-mail.

End Procedure

When you return to the **Business Workplace screen**, you will find that the read e-mail has been automatically transferred to the **Documents subfolder** of the **Inbox folder.** You can transfer it (or any other e-mail) to another folder or delete it entirely by following this next procedure.

Procedure

Storing or Deleting an E-mail Message

Step 1. Click the folder where the e-mail is stored to select and highlight it (Figure 17.20A).

Step 2. The contents of the folder are listed in the **contents panel** (B). Locate the e-mail, and click-and-drag it (C) into another folder, *or*

Click the **Delete button** (D) in the application toolbar of the contents panel to delete the message.

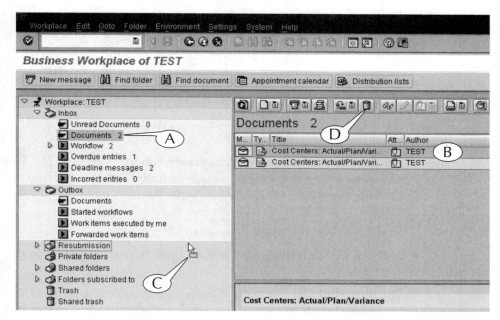

Figure 17.20   Click-and-drag a selected e-mail to another folder, or delete it through the application toolbar of the **contents panel.**

End Procedure

Sending E-mail From the Business Workplace Screen

You can create and send new e-mail and reply to or forward received e-mail from the **Business Workplace screen**. The procedures for these actions are similar to the procedure for e-mailing output reports to other SAP users.

Procedure

Creating and Sending New E-mail

Step 1. Click the **New message button** (A) in the application toolbar of the **Business Workplace screen** (Figure 17.21).

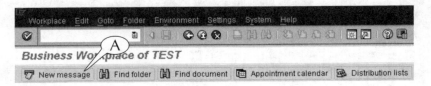

Figure 17.21   Starting new e-mail from the **Business Workplace screen**.

Step 2. The **Create Document and Send screen** appears (Figure 17.22). This is the same screen that you can use to e-mail an output report, *except* that it does not have a tab for the **Attachments subscreen** (because the message has no attachments—yet).

To attach documents to the new e-mail:

- Click the **Attach documents button** (A) in the application toolbar of the screen.

- The **Import file screen** of the *Windows* operating system appears (Figure 17.5A). Locate the document and double-click its name to attach it.

Step 3. Complete the remaining subscreens in the usual way.

- Create a cover letter on the **Document Content subscreen**.

- Define the properties of the e-mail and the attached document on the **Attributes subscreen**.

- Enter the names of recipients and distribution lists on the **Recipient subscreen**.

- Set the conditions for transmitting the e-mail on the **Trans options subscreen**.

Step 4. Click the **Send button** (B) in the application toolbar to send the e-mail.

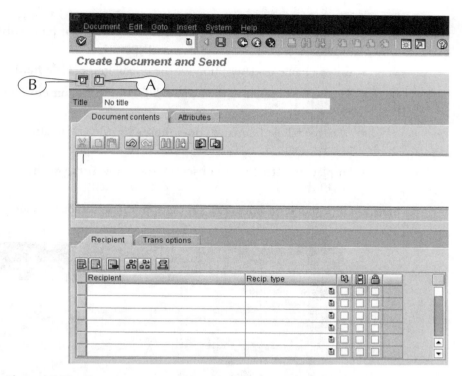

Figure 17.22   Create a new e-mail on the **Create Document and Send screen**.

End Procedure

Procedure

Replying to E-mail

Step 1.   Double-click the line of the e-mail in the **contents panel** of the **Business Workplace screen** (Figure 17.20B).

Step 2.   The **Display Document [Title] screen** appears (Figure 17.23).

- Click the **Reply button** (A) in its application toolbar.

Figure 17.23   Starting a reply to e-mail.

Step 3. The **Create Document screen** appears (Figure 17.24). It contains only two tabs (A) for two subscreens. The **Document contents subscreen** is displayed by default when the screen appears.

- Enter a name or description for the e-mail in the **Title field** (B).

- Enter a cover letter in the text field (C) of the **Document contents subscreen**.

- *Optional:* Click the **Attach documents button** (D) to attach documents to the e-mail.

- Display the **Attributes subscreen** (not shown) and define the properties of the e-mail and any attached documents.

Step 4. Click the **Send button** (E) in the application toolbar to send your reply.

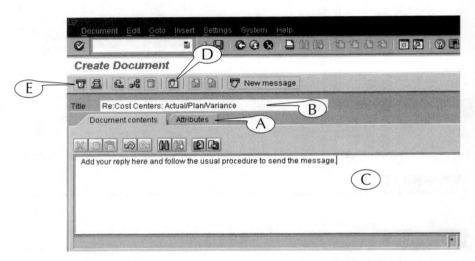

Figure 17.24   Create a cover letter and attach documents to new e-mail on this screen.

End Procedure

Procedure

Forwarding E-mail

Step 1. Display the e-mail in the **contents panel** of the **Business Workplace screen** (Figure 17.25), and click its line once to select and highlight it (A).

Step 2. Click the **Send button** (B) in the application toolbar of the **contents panel**.

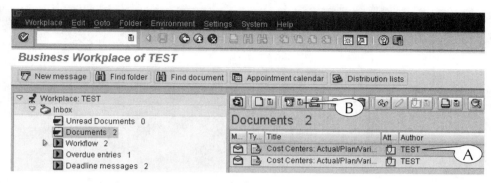

Figure 17.25   First step in forwarding e-mail.

Step 3. The **Send Document screen** appears with a line-item table for entering the names of recipients and distribution lists (Figure 17.26). Follow the procedure for entering these data, which was described earlier in this lesson.

Step 4. Click the **Send mail button** (A) at the bottom of this screen to forward the e-mail to its recipients.

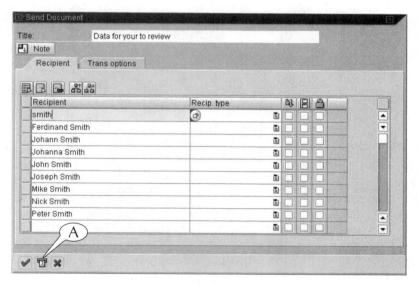

Figure 17.26   Enter the names of the recipients on this screen.

End Procedure

Coda
THE BASIC TRANSACTION TYPES

"A simplistic but comprehensible model is better than a precise but incomprehensible one." — *Patrick Domenico (American scientist)*

The lessons in this book provide instructions on the general use of SAP. They describe procedures that are universal to this system: that is, procedures that can be used in every module and on all transactions, regardless of their specific purposes.

We close this book with a final lesson about the transactions themselves. When you look through the SAP menu folders of the **SAP Easy Access screen**, you will see a dizzying array of hundreds of transactions. For the most part, you will probably work with only a handful of them, maybe one or two dozen at most, but nonetheless, you may still wonder, *How will I learn all of these different procedures?*

There are two answers to that question.

First, your employer will probably give you job aids or other help documents that describe the execution of specific transactions in great detail. Job aids are especially helpful in this regard because they show you every screen you will see, every field in which you will enter data, every button you will click from the beginning to the end of a single transaction (see the sample in the Appendix).

Second, you should not be overwhelmed by the number of transactions and seeming complexity of the SAP system, because there is less there than meets the eye—at least, from the vantage point of the typical end-user. When you step back and look at all the transactions, you will see that there are only four general tasks that they can do—that is, there are really only four basic **transaction types**, and nearly every transaction can be classified as one of these four types. Furthermore, once you learn to run one transaction of a given type, you will know how to run all transactions of that type, because they all require you to enter roughly the same data on their initial screens and they all generate roughly the same sort of output.

The four basic transaction types can be grouped into two classes, which we call the *reporting* and *processing transactions*.

The reporting transactions *display objects*—that is, they display the SAP database record for a tangible object (such as a department, piece of equipment, or consumable material), or an activity (such as a work order or purchase requisition)—and *display lists of related objects*. Because they only read the database and do not alter its contents, they are the most commonly executed types of transactions for most end-users.

The processing transactions *create* and *change objects* (that is, their SAP database records). They have a significant impact on the content, and hence quality, of the SAP database. Consequently, they are usually executed only by a select few employees in a company, and most users do not have access or authority to use them.

This book ends with an overview of the four basic transaction types and their common properties and procedures. To illustrate the transaction types, we describe the procedures for displaying, list-displaying, creating, and changing one object: the record for a **plant maintenance order** (or what we call a *work order*), which is typically used by plant managers to track the activities and costs of installing and maintaining equipment.

> The word *coda* is defined as "a concluding musical section that is formally distinct from the main structure, that serves to round out, conclude or summarize and usually has its own interest." It is a fitting term to describe this part of our book, which deals with a subject outside the SAP workflow. In addition, the coda is usually a single note at the end of a musical work that is allowed to ring out freely and which remains in the listener's ear long after the work is concluded. We want this coda to similarly remain in your ear well after you have read this book, because its contents will enable you to work anywhere in SAP and adapt quickly and confidently to any changes in your use of the system.

Transaction Type 1: Displaying an Object

This first transaction type simply displays the entire database record of a single object. To execute it, you must identify only that object to the system, nothing more. Consequently, the initial screens for this type of transaction usually contains only a single data entry field for the object's code (Figure C.1). You enter it there, then hit the **Enter key** on your keyboard to execute the transaction.

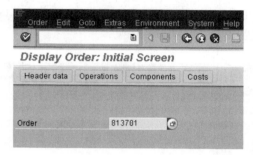

Figure C.1   The initial screen for displaying a work order contains one data field, in which you enter the order number.

The initial screens for displaying purchase requisitions and orders represent a minor variant to this generalization that you might see in some display transactions. When you navigate to the initial screens of these transactions, the system automatically displays the data for the last purchase requisition or order that you worked (Figure C.2). The code for this object appears at the top of the screen (A).

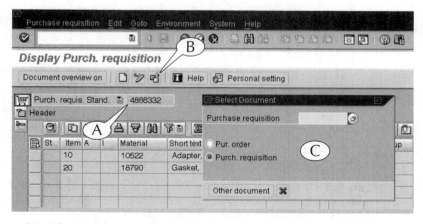

Figure C.2   The initial screen for displaying a purchase requisition or order automatically shows the last requisition or order that you worked. You can change that display through the **Select Document popup screen**.

If this is not the object of immediate interest to you, you can change the display by clicking the **Other requisition** or **Other order button** (B) in the application toolbar. This action calls up the **Select Document popup screen** (C), on which you enter the correct object code (and search for it, if necessary).

The output screens for this transaction type contain large volumes of data. Consequently, the data are usually distributed in multiple field areas, which you can view by scrolling down the length of the output screens, and multiple subscreens, which you can view by clicking their respective tabs (Figure C.3). The data are displayed in gray, read-only data fields, and you cannot alter or customize the output in any way.

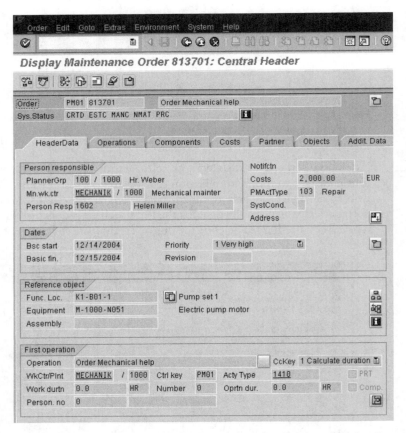

Figure C.3   The output screen for a display of a work order is called the **Central Header screen**. It contains multiple tabbed subscreens and field areas for holding the great volume of data that is recorded for this object.

Transaction Type 2: Displaying a List of Related Objects

This second transaction type displays a list of related objects. The relationship between the objects is defined by **selection criteria**, which you enter on the initial screens of those transactions. These selection criteria consist of one or more specific data entries (either codes or text) for one or more datatypes for that object.

For example, the SAP record for work orders contains hundreds of bits of data of all types, such as the equipment being installed or maintained; the physical plant responsible for the work; the status and nature of the work; and the dates when it was done. Consequently, the initial screen for a *list display* of related work orders contains data entry fields and selection boxes for all these possible selection criteria (Figure C.4).

The simplest way to use this sort of screen is to state your objective for this transaction, find the data entry fields and selection boxes that correspond to that objective, and enter your selection criteria there. Here are three real life examples.

- You are the manager of a physical plant, and you want to know how many work orders are awaiting action by your work crew (described by SAP as *outstanding* in status) or being done by them (or *in process* in status).

    To set up this transaction for this purpose, you would select the *Outstanding* and *In-process order statuses* (A) and enter your plant code in the **Planning Plant field** (B).

- You are a quality control manager, and you have heard from a plant manager that transformer X (which is installed at seven sites in their district) requires much more maintenance work than transformer Y (which is installed at five sites). You want to research the maintenance histories of these 12 devices.

    To set up this transaction, you would select all the available order statuses (A) and enter the codes for the 12 devices on the multiple selection screen for the **Equipment field** (C).

- You are the vice-president in charge of all the physical plants in your company, and you are planning the budget for next year. You want to create a list of all work orders conducted last year by these plants.

    To set up this transaction, you would select the *Completed order status* (A), enter the codes for all the plants on the multiple selection screen of the **Planning Plant field** (B), and enter the dates for the past year in the **Period field** (D).

The initial screens of list-display transactions are especially amenable to the application of screen variants (see Lesson 13). You can use this technique to hide

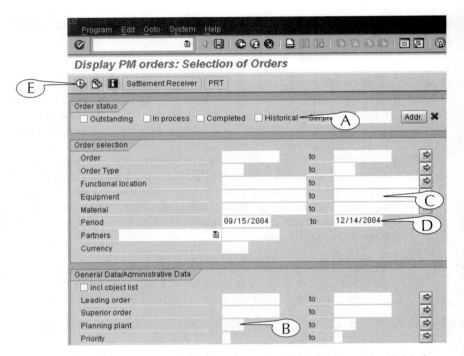

Figure C.4   The initial screen for list-displays of work orders contains fields for every type of data that is collected for this object. Fortunately, you have to enter your selection criteria in only a small number of these fields.

those data fields that you never use and to prepopulate fields with codes that you always enter when you run this transaction.

Once you set up the initial screen for this transaction type, you execute it by clicking the **Execute button** (E) in its application toolbar.

The output screens for this transaction type display their data in the form of line-item reports (Figure C.5). Each line displays by default a few columns of data on a single object that matches all your selection criteria. You can display the database record of one of these objects by double-clicking its code. For this example, this action would call up the **Central Header screen** for a work order (Figure C.3), on which all its data are displayed.

The default versions of these line-item reports do not usually show much useful data, because the developers who set it up could not anticipate the varied needs of its many users. However, the reports can be customized with filters, sorts, sums, and display variants (see Part IV), so that they display data that are relevant to the problem at hand.

For example, the vice-president in our third example could create a display variant that

- Displays the plant code for each order, and groups the line items by this code;

- Displays the actual costs for each work order, and subtotals this value for each plant.

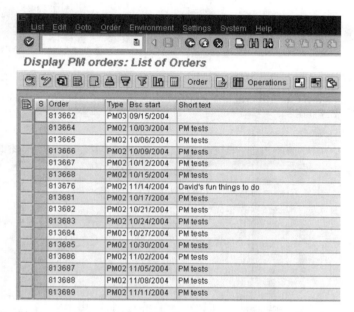

Figure C.5   The output screen for a list-display transaction is a line-item report, in which each row displays data about one object that meets your selection criteria.

Transaction Type 3: Creating an Object

This third transaction type creates the database records for objects. The screens for this type of transaction (and there are often two or more) usually look exactly like the output screens of the corresponding display transactions except that they contain *white* fields in which you must enter new technical and logistical data on the objects (Figure C.6 and Figure C.7).

However, it is impossible for us to outline general rules about working on such initial screens, for the simple reason that every company collects different types of data on objects. In the case of the screens for creating work orders (Figure C.7),

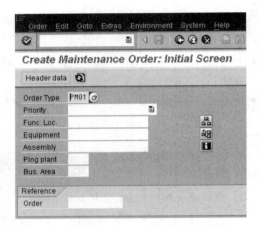

Figure C.6   To create a work order, you must first enter the order type on this initial screen.

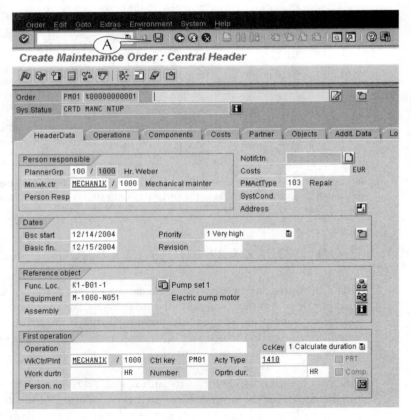

Figure C.7   Once you enter the order type on the first initial screen, this second screen appears with more blank fields for more data about the work order.

for instance, we know one company in which Department A requires its users to enter data only on the **Header Data subscreen** and no other, but Department B requires data entries on the **HeaderData, Operations**, and **Components subscreens**.

To set up these transactions, you must rely on job aids from your company, and you must follow the rules or *protocols* that they define. Once the initial screens are set up by these rules, you create the object by clicking the **Save button** in the standard toolbar (Figure C.7A). If you exit the transaction without clicking this button, all your entries are lost.

The Save action returns you to the first initial screen, where you will find a confirmation that the object was created, along with its object code (Figure C.8). This is the only output of this transaction type.

Order saved with number 813701

Figure C.8   Once you save the data about the work order, you are returned to the initial screen of the transaction, where you receive confirmation of your actions and the new order number in its status bar.

Transaction Type 4: Changing an Object

This fourth transaction type displays the entire database record of a single object *and* allows you to change it if you are authorized to do so.

This transaction type is very similar in its design and operation to the first type. For example, you must identify the object in question to the system on the **Initial screen**, on which you will find a single data field for its code (Figure C.9). You enter it, then hit the **Enter key** on your keyboard to execute the transaction.

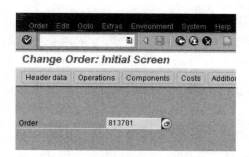

Figure C.9   The **Initial screen** for changing a work order contains one data field, in which you enter the order number.

Similarly, the output screens for this transaction type usually display their large volumes of data in several field areas and on several subscreens. However, the data are displayed in *white* data entry fields, so you can edit them (Figure C.10).

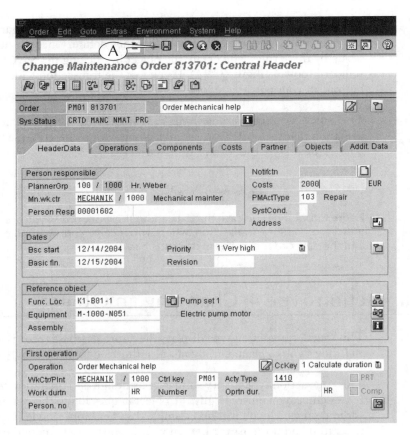

Figure C.10   Change any data entries on the **Central Header screen**, then click the **Save button** to record them.

Once you make any changes, click the **Save button** in the standard toolbar (A) to record your changes and return to the initial screen, where you will find confirmation of your action in the status bar (Figure C.11). Once again, if you don't save at the end of this transaction, all your changes are lost.

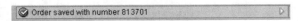

Figure C.11   You receive confirmation of your actions on the initial screen of the transaction. However, the order number remains the same.

Once again, the initial screens for changing purchase requisitions and orders represent a minor variant to this generalization. When you navigate to the initial screens of these transactions, the system automatically displays the data for the last requisition or order that you worked. If this is not the object of interest to you, click the **Other requisition** or **Other order button** (see Figure C.2B), which will again appear in the application toolbar, and then enter the correct object code on the **Select Document popup screen** (see Figure C.2C).

Appendix: SAP 4.7 Job Aids
Create a Plant Maintenance Order (IW31)

Plant maintenance (or **PM**) **orders** are created in SAP 4.7 to track the activities and costs of installing and maintaining technical equipment. This job aid describes the procedures for creating PM orders in accordance with the policies and protocols of our company.

To execute this transaction, you need to know

- The SAP object code for the equipment in question
- The employee number of the manager of the plant which is responsible for that equipment

Procedure

Step 1. Enter the T-code **IW31** in the **command field** (A) of the **SAP Easy Access screen**, then hit the **Enter key** on your keyboard, *or*

Follow the menu path

Logistics > Plant Maintenance > Maintenance Processing > Orders > Create (General)

or

Open your **Favorites folder** and click the link to this transaction (if it is there).

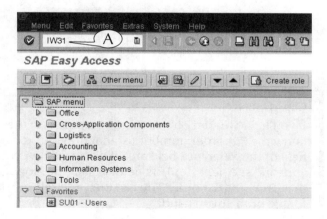

Step 2. The **Create Maintenance Order: Initial screen** appears.

- Enter a type code in the **Order Type field** (A). The code consists of a two-character work descriptor followed by a two-character expense descriptor. There are three possible work descriptor codes:
  - **PM**: for routine preventive maintenance of an otherwise functioning object.
  - **SC**: for emergency repairs due to storms and catastrophic events
  - **CM**: for corrective maintenance of an object that is working at less-than-peak levels

  There are two possible expense descriptors:
  - **01**: for maintenance of existing equipment.
  - **02**: for installation of new equipment.

- Enter a priority code in the **Priority field** (B). Use the list menu icon to select from a list of codes.

- Enter the equipment number in the **Equipment field** (C).

- Hit the **Enter key** on your keyboard.

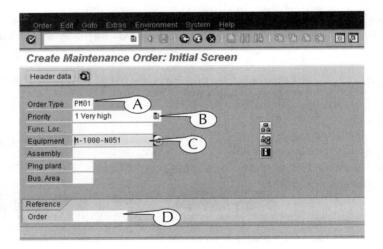

Copy Data from a Previous Order

If you have worked on this same equipment in the recent past and know the PM order number for that previous job, enter it in the **Order field** of the **Reference field area** (D). When the **Central Header screen** appears (see next step), its fields will be prepopulated with data from that previous PM order. You can then edit select fields to update them for the problem on hand.

Step 3. The **Create Maintenance Order: Central Header screen** appears.

- Enter a brief description of the problem in the **Short text field** (A).

- Enter a maintenance activity type code in the **PMActType field** (B).

- Enter an estimated finish date for the work in the **Basic fin field** (C).

- Enter the employee ID number for the manager of the plant responsible for the equipment in the **Person no field** (D).

- Hit the **Enter key** on your keyboard.

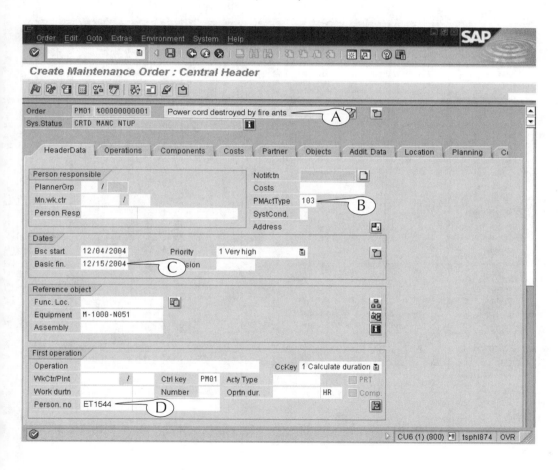

Step 4. The system draws from the database record for the equipment and plant manager and populates other critical fields with data on the maintenance plant and functional location.

- Click the **Save button** (A).

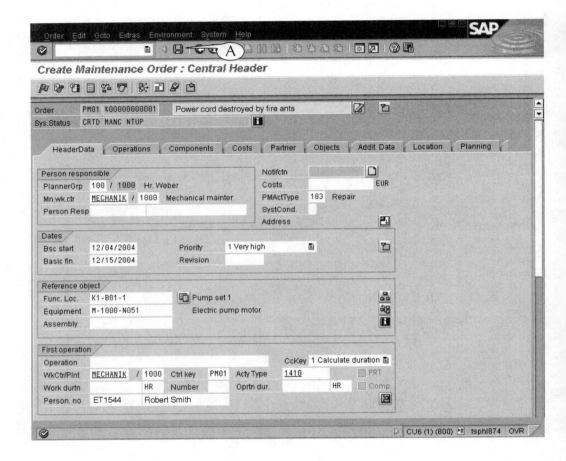

Step 5. The initial screen returns with a message in its status bar that the order is created (A).

- Record the order number.

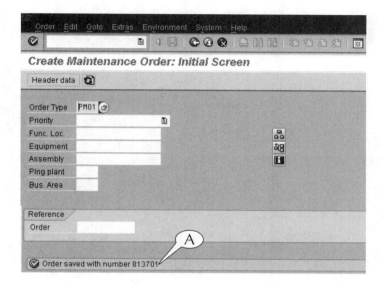

INDEX

THIS BOOK IS SAFARI ENABLED

INCLUDES FREE 45-DAY ACCESS TO THE ONLINE EDITION

The Safari® Enabled icon on the cover of your favorite technology book means the book is available through Safari Bookshelf. When you buy this book, you get free access to the online edition for 45 days.

Safari Bookshelf is an electronic reference library that lets you easily search thousands of technical books, find code samples, download chapters, and access technical information whenever and wherever you need it.

TO GAIN 45-DAY SAFARI ENABLED ACCESS TO THIS BOOK:

- Go to **http://www.phptr.com/safarienabled**
- Complete the brief registration form
- Enter the coupon code found in the front of this book on the "Copyright" page

If you have difficulty registering on Safari Bookshelf or accessing the online edition, please e-mail customer-service@safaribooksonline.com.